WINDOWS
ON·THE·WORLD

WONDERS
·OF·THE·
WORLD

Giovanni Caselli

Contributing Illustrators:
Mark Bergin
Nicholas Hewetson
John James

DORLING KINDERSLEY · LONDON

Editor Susan Mennell
Series Editor Angela Wilkes
Series Art Editor Roger Priddy

Editorial Director Jackie Douglas
Art Director Roger Bristow

First published in Great Britain in 1988
by Dorling Kindersley Publishers Limited,
9 Henrietta Street, London WC2E 8PS

Copyright © 1988 Dorling Kindersley
Limited, London

British Library Cataloguing in Publication Data
Caselli, Giovanni
    Wonders of the world.—(Windows on the
world).
    1. Structures of historical importance.
For children
    I. Title   II. Series
    624

    ISBN 0-86318-309-3

Phototypeset by Southern Positives and Negatives (SPAN)
Reproduced in Singapore by Colourscan
Printed in Spain by Artes Garficas, Toledo S.A.
D.L.TO:370-1988

CONTENTS

THE SEVEN WONDERS OF THE WORLD

Over 2,000 years ago, a Greek writer called Antipater of Sidon, compiled a list of what he considered to be the most spectacular buildings of his day. These later became widely known as the Seven Wonders of the World. Nobody knows exactly why Antipater made his list. Perhaps it was intended as an early tourist guide to the countries of the eastern Mediterranean.

The actual number of "wonders" is thought to be significant. Since earliest times the number seven was considered sacred and was often associated in folklore and religion with special or mystical events.

Inevitably, over the centuries, some of the Seven Wonders collapsed and fell into ruins, so that later writers compiled their own lists of other splendid sights or "wonders".

But what distinguishes all the "wonders" from other buildings throughout history, whether ancient or modern, is that there is something amazing about them – either their colossal size, the remarkable way in which they were built, or simply their outstanding beauty. And the one factor they all have in common is their unfailing ability to make people marvel at their very existence.

Finding a wonder
On this map you can spot the original Seven Wonders of the World. Each building has been drawn in its exact location so that you can see where the ancient "wonders" were situated in relation to each other.

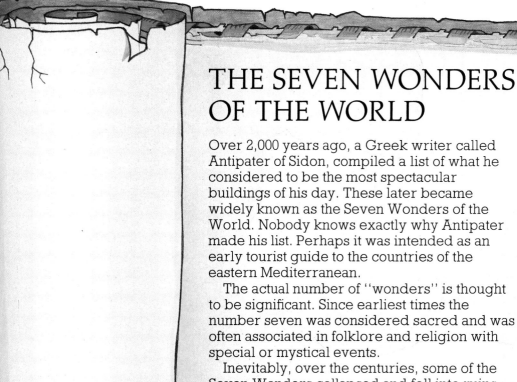

Mediterranean Sea

The book of revelations

This book is divided into seven chapters, based around the Seven Wonders of the World. Each chapter opens with an artist's impression of an ancient wonder and goes on to explain why and how it was built. Comparisons are made with later buildings, often highlighting striking resemblances between the ancient and modern.

4

The first chapter tells of the pyramids of Egypt and other big constructions, such as Stonehenge.

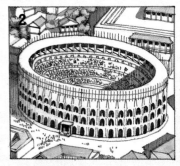

Chapter 2 compares the Hanging Gardens with entertainment centres, like the Colosseum.

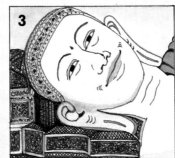

The third chapter looks at the Statue of Zeus and other shrines, such as this Buddha in Burma.

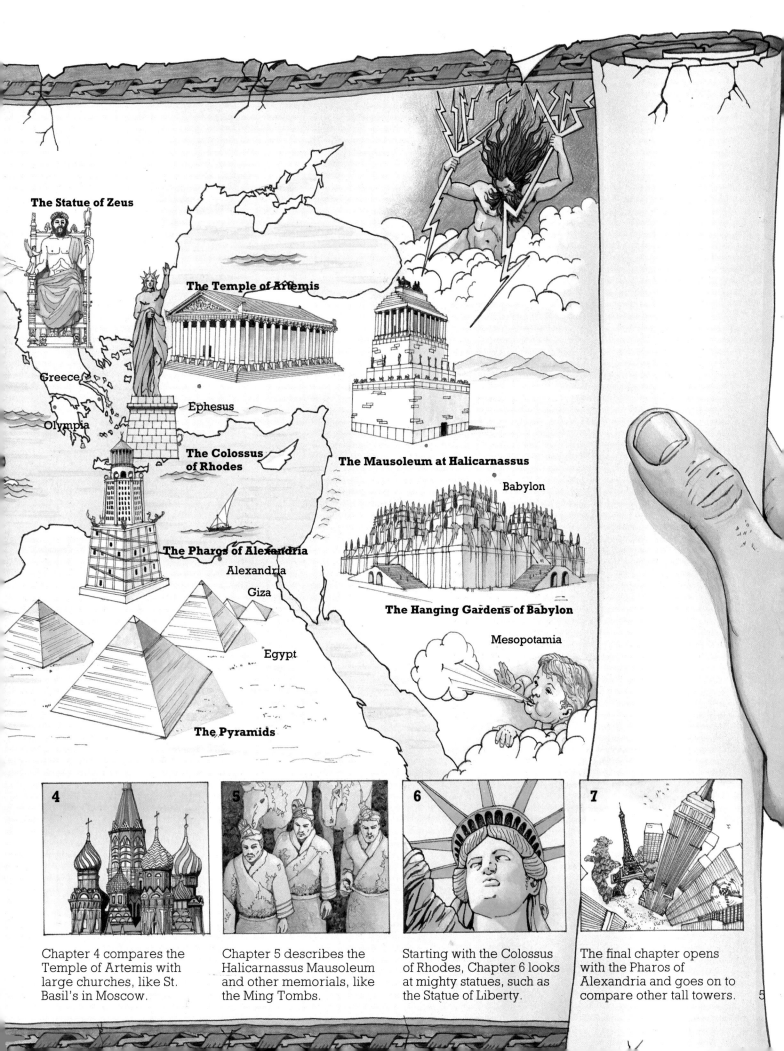

The Statue of Zeus

The Temple of Artemis

The Mausoleum at Halicarnassus

The Colossus of Rhodes

The Pharos of Alexandria

The Hanging Gardens of Babylon

The Pyramids

Greece

Olympia

Ephesus

Alexandria

Giza

Egypt

Babylon

Mesopotamia

4
Chapter 4 compares the Temple of Artemis with large churches, like St. Basil's in Moscow.

5
Chapter 5 describes the Halicarnassus Mausoleum and other memorials, like the Ming Tombs.

6
Starting with the Colossus of Rhodes, Chapter 6 looks at mighty statues, such as the Statue of Liberty.

7
The final chapter opens with the Pharos of Alexandria and goes on to compare other tall towers.

1 THE PYRAMIDS

Towering above the desert, near the banks of the River Nile, stand the famous pyramids of Egypt. Built by the Ancient Egyptians nearly 5,000 years ago, they are the oldest of the seven ancient wonders of the world and the only one that has remained standing to the present day.

The pyramids were built as tombs for the kings of Ancient Egypt. The Ancient Egyptians believed in life after death, so to make sure that their kings had everything they might need in their next life, they buried many personal treasures alongside them. In the burial chambers of pyramids archaeologists have found jewels, food, furniture, musical instruments and hunting equipment.

A mammoth task
The largest and most impressive of the pyramids is the Great Pyramid at Giza. Completed in 2580 B.C. for King Cheops, it took thousands of men about 30 years to build.

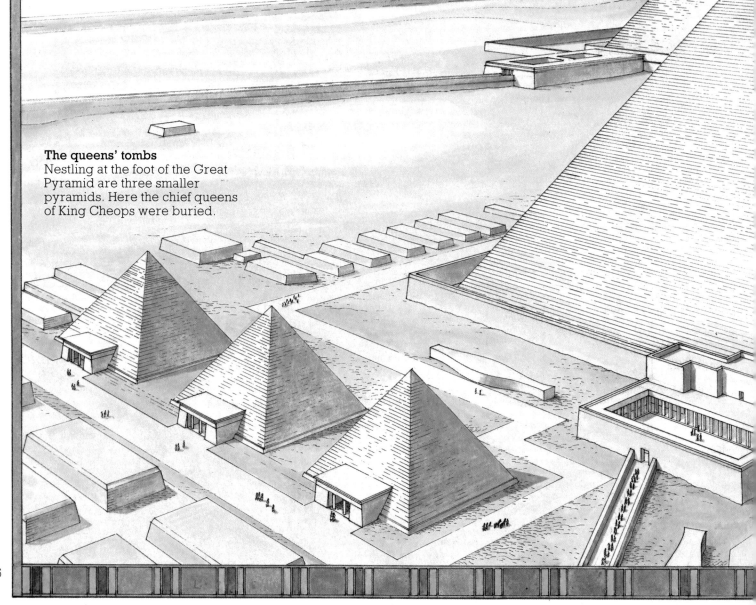

The queens' tombs
Nestling at the foot of the Great Pyramid are three smaller pyramids. Here the chief queens of King Cheops were buried.

Reaching for the sky
The Great Pyramid rises to a height of about 137m (449ft) and each side measures 230m (755ft) at its base. The pyramid was made of about 2 million blocks of stone, each weighing about 2,300kg (5,074lb).

BUILDING THE PYRAMIDS

The pyramids were built without any machines and with the aid of only a few simple tools. The men who built them were not slaves, but skilled workers and peasants who worked on the pyramids during the months when the Nile flooded the fields and made farming impossible.

The pyramids were built in stages. First the site was levelled, then a surveyor took a bearing from the stars to work out the position of the square base, so that the four sides faced north, south, east and west.

Once the foundations were laid, the wall was built, using huge blocks of stone cut from distant quarries and ferried across the Nile. Finally the pyramid was encased in white limestone.

Taking shape
The Ancient Egyptians built their pyramids from the centre outwards. Here you can see workers toiling to construct the Great Pyramid at Giza.

Where are the pyramids?

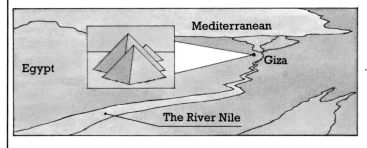

The king's burial chamber

The Great Pyramid

King's burial chamber

Passageway

The king was buried in the heart of the pyramid. His sarcophagus, a type of coffin, was placed in the burial chamber while the side of the pyramid was still being built. The entrance to the chamber was then sealed, but many years later thieves broke in and stole the king's treasures.

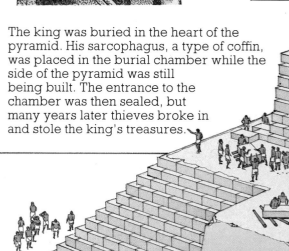

A labour of love
Thousands of stonemasons, carpenters and ordinary labourers worked on the pyramids in return for food and clothes. Everyone wanted to help build the King's tomb, as they considered him to be a god.

Muscle power
No form of wheeled transport was used to move blocks of stone from the quarries to the site of the pyramids. They were lashed to strong sledges and dragged from the boats to the building site.

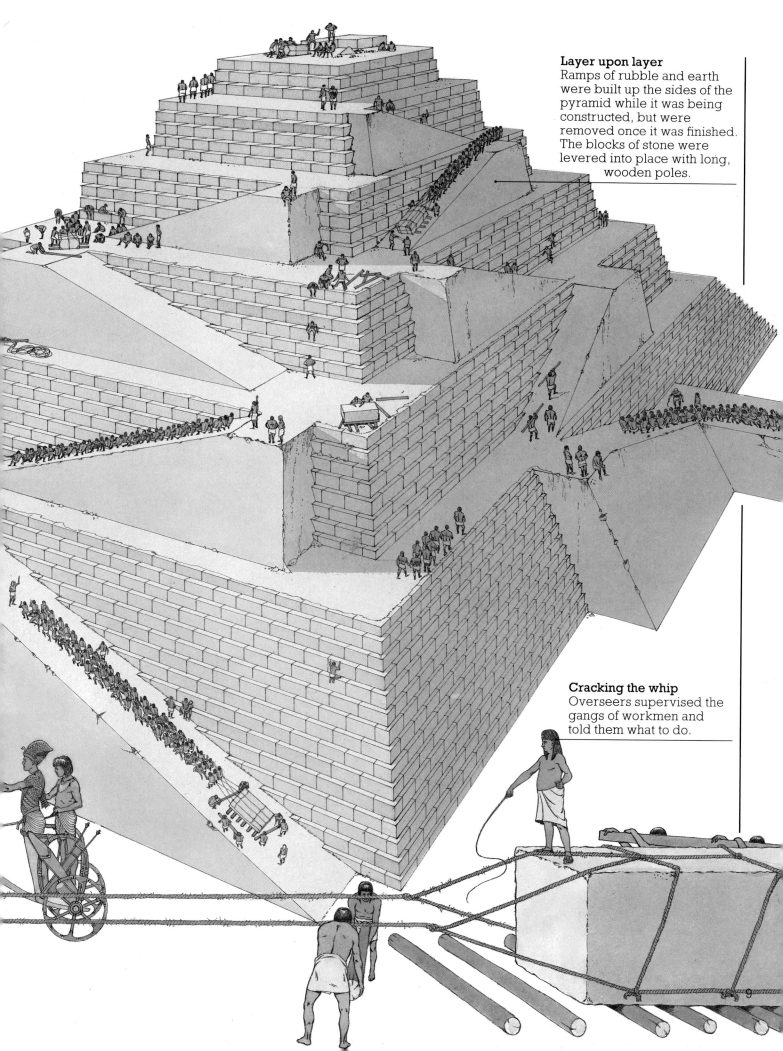

Layer upon layer
Ramps of rubble and earth were built up the sides of the pyramid while it was being constructed, but were removed once it was finished. The blocks of stone were levered into place with long, wooden poles.

Cracking the whip
Overseers supervised the gangs of workmen and told them what to do.

9

OTHER GREAT PYRAMIDS

Although the pyramids built by the Ancient Egyptians are the most famous pyramids, they are not the only ones ever built. Other ancient civilisations also built huge, pyramid-shaped monuments. Most pyramids were some kind of temple dedicated to a god. As in Ancient Egypt, kings were sometimes worshipped as gods and when they died, they were buried in tombs concealed deep inside a pyramid.

Borobodur

The word "Borobodur" means "temple on the hill". Situated on a hill in the jungle of Java in Southeast Asia, Borobodur is the largest Buddhist temple in the world. It was built in about 800 A.D. but was later abandoned after an earthquake and fell into ruins. For centuries the temple lay hidden in the jungle, but in 1814 it was found again and since then archaeologists have restored it to its former glory.

Changing shapes

Borobodur looks like an enormous terraced pyramid. It has a square base above which are several circular terraces that become smaller towards the top. At the very top of the temple, 46m (150ft) above the ground, is a huge bell-shaped shrine or "stupa".

A winding path

The journey to the top involves passing through a maze of stairs and passageways. Adorning the walls are thousands of magnificent carvings showing scenes of life in ancient Java and stories about the life of Buddha.

Seated in a stone cage

Around the large central stupa are about seventy smaller stupas. Inside each one sits a statue of the Buddha, which can be seen through the holes in the protective stone casing.

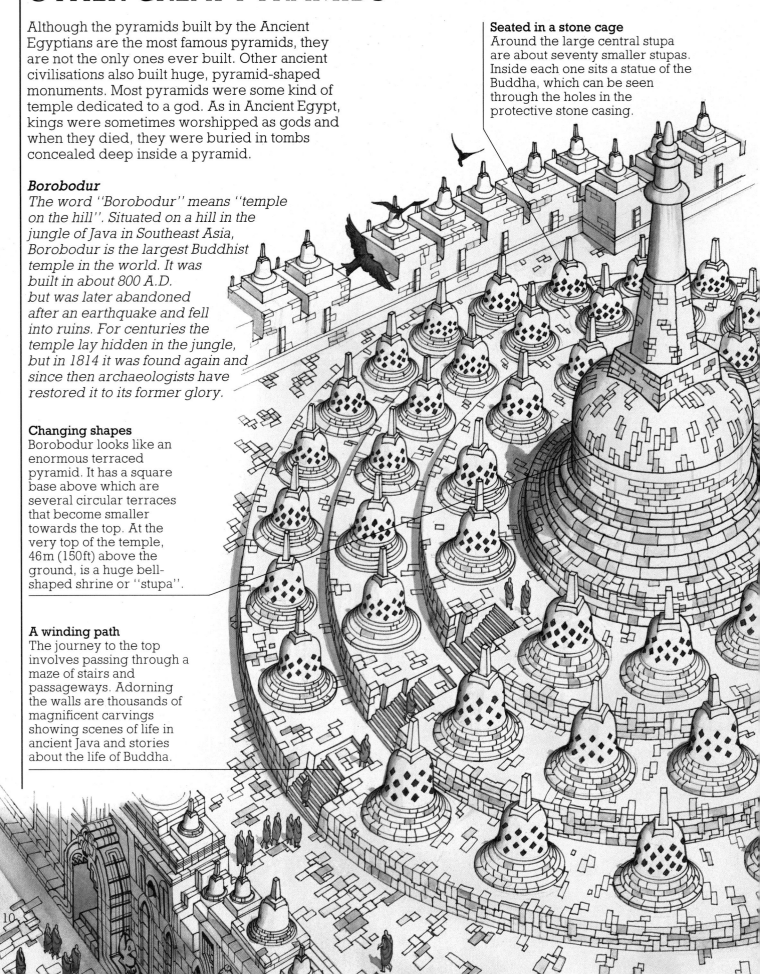

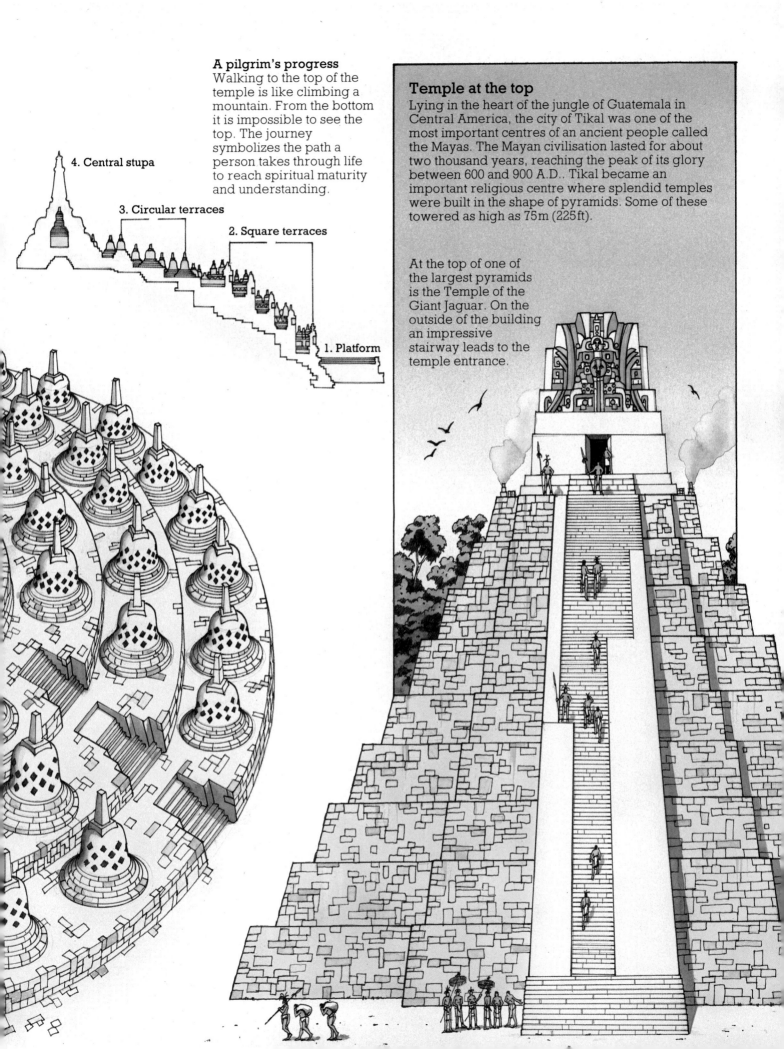

A pilgrim's progress
Walking to the top of the temple is like climbing a mountain. From the bottom it is impossible to see the top. The journey symbolizes the path a person takes through life to reach spiritual maturity and understanding.

4. Central stupa

3. Circular terraces

2. Square terraces

1. Platform

Temple at the top

Lying in the heart of the jungle of Guatemala in Central America, the city of Tikal was one of the most important centres of an ancient people called the Mayas. The Mayan civilisation lasted for about two thousand years, reaching the peak of its glory between 600 and 900 A.D.. Tikal became an important religious centre where splendid temples were built in the shape of pyramids. Some of these towered as high as 75m (225ft).

At the top of one of the largest pyramids is the Temple of the Giant Jaguar. On the outside of the building an impressive stairway leads to the temple entrance.

GREAT STONES OF OUR TIME

Ever since his appearance on Earth, man has shifted enormous stones to build the most amazing constructions, as the Ancient Egyptians did when building the pyramids. In early times, using only the most primitive of tools, men were able to move colossal stones or "megaliths" great distances, then manoeuvre them into the position they wanted. Nowadays, with advanced technology and powerful machines, man is constantly building more sophisticated buildings, dams, bridges and tunnels, but it remains to be seen whether they will stand the test of time like the constructions of our primitive ancestors.

The Great Wall of China
The Great Wall of China is the largest man-made construction in the world. This huge fortification was built to keep out fierce tribes that tried to invade China. Begun in the 3rd century B.C. by the first emperor of China, Shi Huang Ti, the wall took hundreds of years to complete.

Watchtowers
Positioned at regular intervals along the wall are a series of imposing watchtowers and gatehouses. Signals were sent out from the towers, using smoke during the day and fire at night.

Stonehenge
On Salisbury Plain in southwest England stands an ancient circle of standing stones known as Stonehenge, one of the most famous prehistoric sites in the world. Built between 3,000 and 1,500 B.C., the circle measures 30m (97ft) across and is made with massive blocks of stone up to 4m (13.5ft) high.

A mighty feat
The stones found at Stonehenge were probably dragged to the site from quarries 32 km (20 miles) away. Holes were then dug for them and they were heaved into a standing position by teams of men, using primitive levers.

Magic circle
It is a mystery why Stonehenge was built. Some people think it may have been used as the setting for pagan religious ceremonies. Others think the stones may have helped ancient man to follow the movements of the stars.

Itaipu Dam
Situated on the Panama River in southern Brazil, the Itaipu Dam is the largest hydro-electric plant in the world. The South American countries of Brazil and Paraguay joined forces to build the dam in the 1970s. It has an enormous capacity and is expected to generate as much power as the Aswan and Grand Coulee dams combined.

Look out
Built along the crest of a mountain range, the wall formed an effective barrier against invaders. Guards were posted along the wall so that they could raise the alarm if danger threatened.

A long snake
The wall is 2,450km (1,500 miles) long, equivalent to the distance between London and Moscow. It stretches from the mouth of the Yellow Sea to a point deep in Central Asia.

Parallel lines
The wall has two parallel walls that rise to a height of 9m (30ft) on either side of a roadway 3.5m (10ft) wide. Most of the wall is made of stone and earth covered in brick.

A deadly task
Building such a massive barrier in a mountainous region was a difficult task. Countless slaves were used to carry out the work and many thousands died in the process.

2 THE HANGING GARDENS OF BABYLON

Of the seven Wonders of the World, none has fired people's imagination as much as the Hanging Gardens of Babylon. There are no descriptions of them by writers who lived at the time, but stories about them were passed down by word of mouth and the legend grew of an earthly paradise rising out of the desert.

A Roman writer visited the gardens long after the fall of Babylon and found them still standing. He described them as a series of vaulted terraces, built pyramid-like, one on top of another, and flanked by walls 7.6m (25ft) thick. Each terrace contained soil deep enough for trees to grow.

A green pyramid
Exotic plants and flowers cascaded over the terraces. Cypress trees and palms provided shade and the air was heavy with the scent of aromatic plants and flowers.

For the love of a wife
The gardens were built by Semiramis in the 9th century B.C. on the orders of King Nebuchadnezzar. The King created the gardens for his wife, Amytis, who missed the green and hilly landscape of her homeland. The lush gardens provided a cool refuge from the burning heat of the desert in which Babylon stood and many people visited them.

Watering the garden
In order to irrigate the gardens, water was pumped from the nearby River Euphrates through a hidden network of pipes leading to the terraces.

THE CITY OF BABYLON

The ancient city of Babylon lay on the banks of the River Euphrates in the fertile land of Mesopotamia, known today as Iraq. Renowned for its Hanging Gardens and for its defensive outer walls, which many considered to be a Wonder of the World in their own right, Babylon was one of the wealthiest cities of the ancient world. It was a centre both of learning and commerce, where merchants from faraway lands came to trade in exotic spices and precious goods.

The city reached the height of its power under King Nebuchadnezzar, who reigned from 605 to 562 B.C. But the city's golden age was not to last. In 539 B.C. the Persians took control of the city and Babylon lost its independence for ever. As the years went by, people left the city and by 200 A.D. it was deserted and in ruins.

City sights
Visitors to Babylon marvelled at its sights. From the heart of the city rose the towering ziggurat and a temple devoted to Marduk, the patron god of Babylon. Nearby were the Hanging Gardens and the magnificent royal palace.

A grand entrance
The magnificent Ishtar Gate was the main entrance to the city. Dedicated to the goddess Ishtar, it was covered in glazed blue tiles decorated with pictures of dragons and other mythical beasts. There is a reconstruction of the Ishtar Gate in the Berlin Museum.

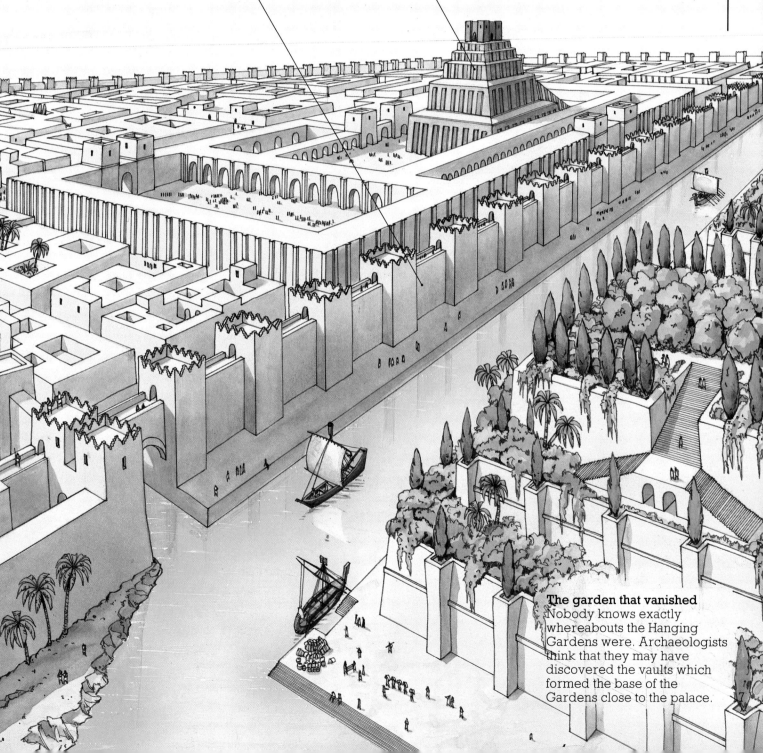

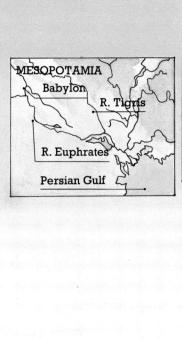

MESOPOTAMIA

Babylon

R. Tigris

R. Euphrates

Persian Gulf

A walled city
The city was encircled by a massive double wall with eight great gateways. Between the outer battlements ran a raised roadway wide enough for four-horse chariots to drive along it.

The Tower of Babel?
The ziggurat was a terraced pyramid-like tower 90m (300ft) tall. At the top of it was a temple. Some historians think the ziggurat may have been the legendary Tower of Babel in the Bible.

Remains of the past
Today nothing is left of Babylon apart from a few ruins. Archaeologists have excavated the main street and think they have discovered the foundations of the ziggurat and the royal palace.

The garden that vanished
Nobody knows exactly whereabouts the Hanging Gardens were. Archaeologists think that they may have discovered the vaults which formed the base of the Gardens close to the palace.

17

ENTERTAINMENT FOR THE PEOPLE

Like the Hanging Gardens of Babylon, the Colosseum in Rome was built for the entertainment of the people. On public holidays, Romans flocked to this massive sports arena to watch fierce gladiator fights.

Work began on the Colosseum in A.D. 70 and was completed 12 years later. It was a masterpiece of engineering. Formed like two Greek theatres put together, the amphitheatre was oval in shape to give spectators a good view of the fights. The Romans used movable scaffolding so that the huge workforce of slaves could work on the whole building at once. They also used concrete (which they invented) and metal frames to strengthen it.

The Colosseum is now in ruins, but even though over half of it has disappeared, it is still the greatest monument of Ancient Rome.

A day at the fights

Here you have a bird's-eye view of the Colosseum. Spectators are thronging to the entrances and down in the arena bloodthirsty fights are already in progress. Part of the amphitheatre is cut away so you can see the passageways beneath the arena.

A giant building
The Colosseum is huge, rising to a height of 50m (159ft) and measuring 527m (nearly a third of a mile) all the way round. Its four storeys were originally shaded from the sun by a huge awning.

Thousands of spectators
The amphitheatre could hold up to 50,000 people, each of whom had a numbered seat. There were 80 public entrances, so the building could be emptied quickly. The Emperor had his own entrance.

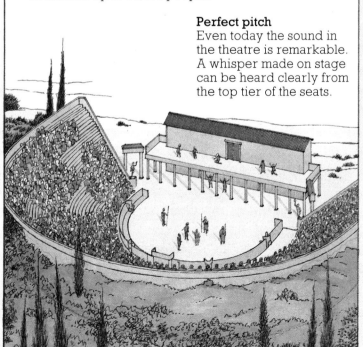

The theatre at Epidaurus

One of the main forms of entertainment for the Ancient Greeks was going to see a play. These were performed in vast, open-air theatres, like this one that has been restored at Epidaurus in Greece. Built into a mountainside, the steep auditorium could seat up to 14,000 people.

Perfect pitch
Even today the sound in the theatre is remarkable. A whisper made on stage can be heard clearly from the top tier of the seats.

The spectators' galleries
The galleries rose in tiers.
The Emperor and V.I.P.s
had the best seats, close to
the arena. Knights and
wealthy citizens sat on the
next two levels and
ordinary people sat at the
top of the amphitheatre.

Fighting for their life
Gladiators were prisoners of war,
criminals or slaves condemned to
death. They were trained to fight in
special schools and the Games gave
them a chance to win their freedom.
If a gladiator fought well, the Emperor
or the crowd gave him the "thumbs
up" sign and he was pardoned. If he
was defeated and given the "thumbs
down" sign, he was killed on the spot.

There were different types of
gladiator. Some fought with a net and
trident, some with a bow and arrow
and others with a sword and shield.
Another type fought on horseback.

One of the most spectacular fights at
the Colosseum took the form of a mock
sea battle. The arena was flooded and
gladiators fought each other from
boats or in the water.

The field of combat
The arena was a wooden
floor covered with sand.
Scenery was hoisted up
from below by pulleys.
Beneath the arena was a
maze of passages, chambers
and the animals' dens.

Some gladiators had to fight against
wild animals, such as lions and tigers.
At the end of the fights any dead
bodies were removed and sand
spread over the blood on the ground.

PALACES OF PLEASURE AND LEARNING

In the last few decades some spectacular new buildings have been constructed as multi-purpose cultural centres. These house facilities for different kinds of activity all under one roof – stages for plays, concerts and spectacles, often as well as museums, art galleries and libraries. The idea of these centres is to provide places where people can enjoy hours of pleasure in many different ways without the constrictions often associated with traditional museums, art galleries and theatres.

Although many of these arts centres are large, they are not renowned for their size but for their beauty and the originality of their architecture. Competitions are often held to find a unique design for a new centre and the resulting buildings, like the Pompidou Centre in Paris and the Sydney Opera House, stand out from their surroundings and become local landmarks. They are the "Wonders" of our own age and attract phenomenal numbers of visitors each year.

The Pompidou Centre
This striking centre of art and culture was opened in 1977. Right in the heart of Paris, it houses a museum of modern art, a library and areas for dance, films and other activities.

A building inside out
To keep as much free space as possible inside the Pompidou Centre, the architects designed it with all its working parts on the outside of the building – like a body with all its inner organs on show, including the skeleton.

Colour coding
The building was assembled like a giant toy construction kit, with different colours for each part (not all of which you can see here). The framework is white, the air conditioning system blue, the water pipes green, the lifts red and the electrical parts yellow.

Continuing outside
In front of the Centre is a big square where all sorts of open-air entertainments go on. As the Centre's escalators and walkways are in transparent tubes on the front of the building, its visitors can watch what is happening in the square.

The Sydney Opera House

A space age fantasy in concrete, the Sydney Opera House is one of Australia's most famous landmarks. Its brilliant white roof rises like sails above Sydney Harbour.

Designed by Jorn Utzon, a Danish architect, the Opera House was eventually opened in 1973. It had taken 14 years to build and had cost a fortune, but has been very successful.

The Opera House is not really an opera house at all, but a centre for performing arts. Its four halls are used for concerts, opera and ballet, theatre and other activities.

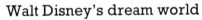

Walt Disney's dream world

The EPCOT* Centre in Disneyworld, Florida, was planned by Walt Disney to be a domed, pollution-free city. It is now a theme park tracing man's progress through the age of communications. Its dramatic gateway, shown here, is a giant sphere nearly 17 storeys high, called Spaceship Earth.

*Experimental Prototype Community of Tomorrow

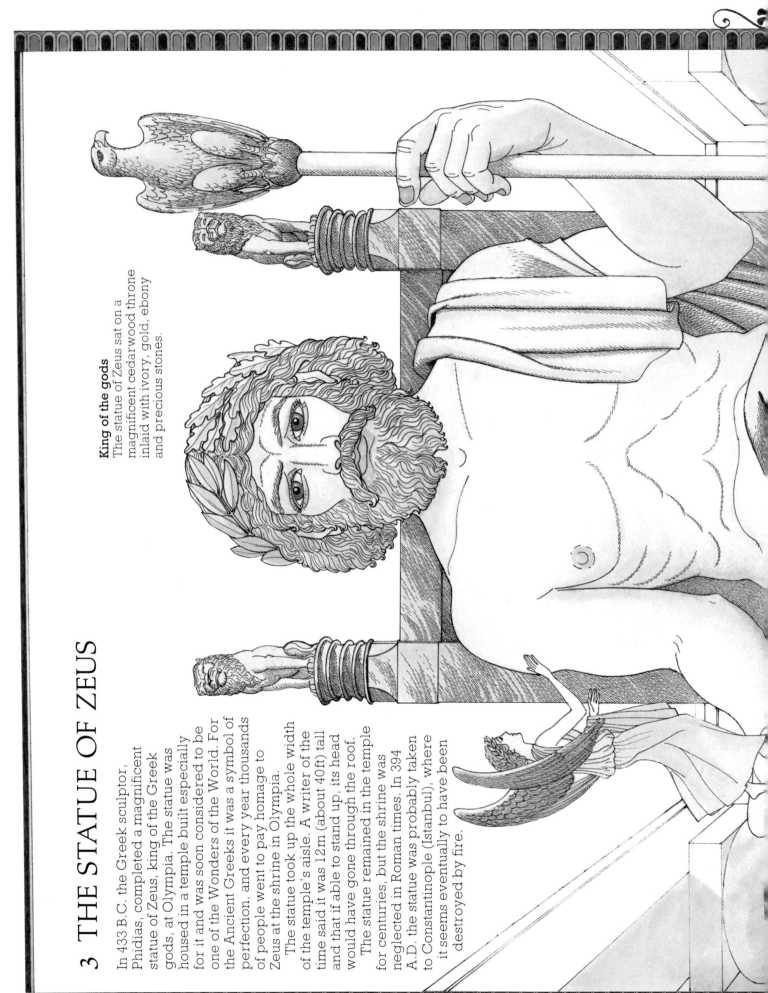

3 THE STATUE OF ZEUS

In 433 B.C. the Greek sculptor, Phidias, completed a magnificent statue of Zeus, king of the Greek gods, at Olympia. The statue was housed in a temple built especially for it and was soon considered to be one of the Wonders of the World. For the Ancient Greeks it was a symbol of perfection, and every year thousands of people went to pay homage to Zeus at the shrine in Olympia.

The statue took up the whole width of the temple's aisle. A writer of the time said it was 12m (about 40ft) tall and that if able to stand up, its head would have gone through the roof.

The statue remained in the temple for centuries, but the shrine was neglected in Roman times. In 394 A.D. the statue was probably taken to Constantinople (Istanbul), where it seems eventually to have been destroyed by fire.

King of the gods
The statue of Zeus sat on a magnificent cedarwood throne inlaid with ivory, gold, ebony and precious stones.

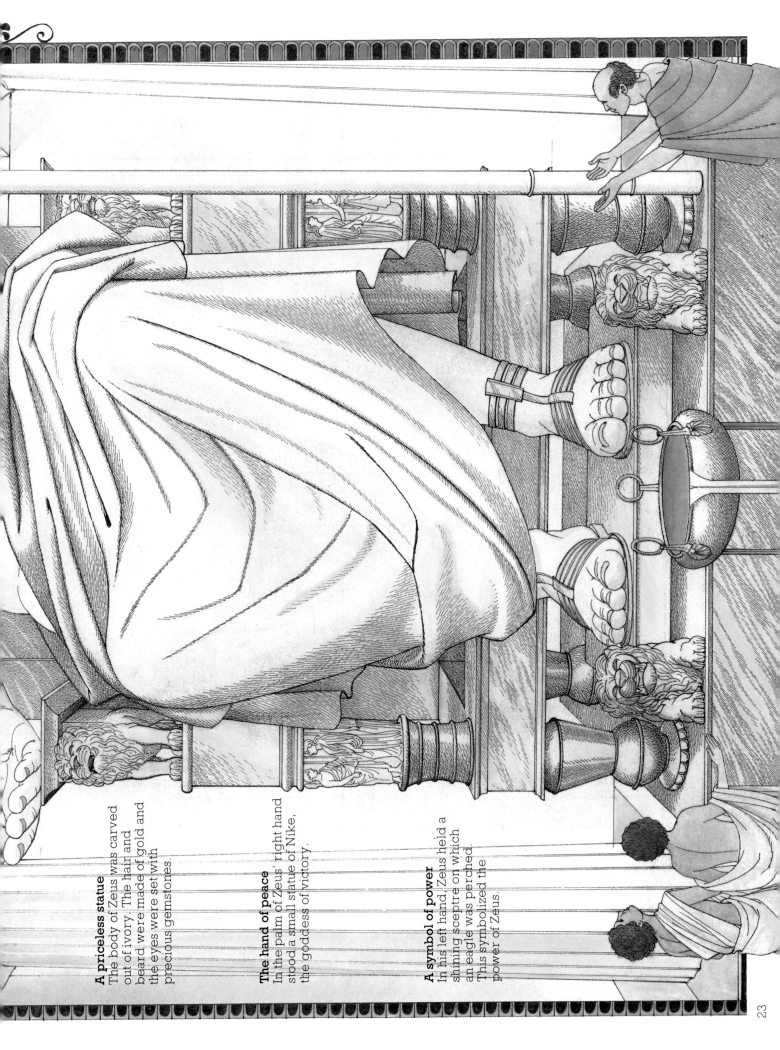

A priceless statue
The body of Zeus was carved out of ivory. The hair and beard were made of gold and the eyes were set with precious gemstones.

The hand of peace
In the palm of Zeus' right hand stood a small statue of Nike, the goddess of victory.

A symbol of power
In his left hand, Zeus held a shining sceptre on which an eagle was perched. This symbolized the power of Zeus.

OLYMPIA AND THE GAMES

Mount Olympus, the highest mountain in Greece, was believed by the Ancient Greeks to be the home of Zeus, king of the gods. For centuries, Zeus was worshipped at Olympia and by the 5th century B.C. it was one of the most important holy places in Greece. The Temple of Zeus, begun in 470 B.C., took 15 years to complete.

But Olympia was not only famous for its temples. The first Olympic Games were held there in 776 B.C.. Every four years all wars were suspended as athletes gathered at Olympia to compete.

A sanctuary for the gods
The city of Olympia had two different areas. One part, the "altis", was a sacred grove dedicated to the gods. The other area was where people carried out their daily affairs. According to legend, Hercules, the son of Zeus, founded Olympia.

In pursuit of excellence
Athletes came from all over Greece to compete in the Games. Every athlete wanted to do his best in honour of the gods. The Games had strict rules and athletes who broke them were punished.

A mighty temple
One of the largest temples of its day, the Temple of Zeus was over 64m (210ft) long and 18.3m (60ft) high. Its columns were over 9.7m (32ft) high. It was eventually destroyed by a series of earthquakes in the 6th century A.D..

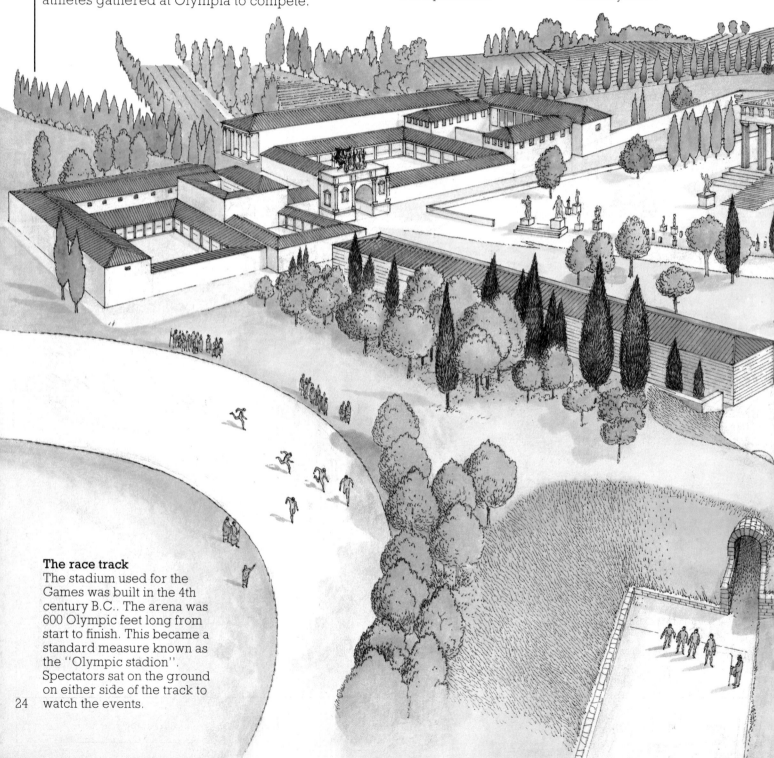

The race track
The stadium used for the Games was built in the 4th century B.C.. The arena was 600 Olympic feet long from start to finish. This became a standard measure known as the "Olympic stadion". Spectators sat on the ground on either side of the track to watch the events.

The Greek gods

The Ancient Greeks believed in a "family" of gods, blessed with eternal youth, that had complete control over the lives of ordinary people. Zeus was the king of the gods and reigned over his family, some of whom are on the right. Each god or goddess had his or her own special role and temples were built for the most important amongst them.

Poseidon   Hephaestus   Zeus   Hera   Ares   Hermes

Athena   Demeter   Aphrodite   Apollo   Hestia   Artemis

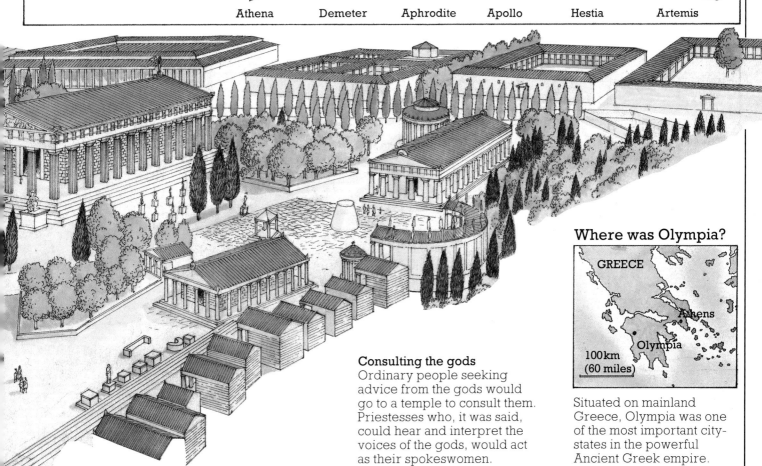

Consulting the gods

Ordinary people seeking advice from the gods would go to a temple to consult them. Priestesses who, it was said, could hear and interpret the voices of the gods, would act as their spokeswomen.

Where was Olympia?

GREECE

Athens

Olympia

100km
(60 miles)

Situated on mainland Greece, Olympia was one of the most important city-states in the powerful Ancient Greek empire.

Sportsmanship

At first, the Olympic Games consisted of a simple race, but as the years went by, more events were added and athletes could participate in all the sports shown below, as well as chariot racing and the pentathlon (five combined events). The games lasted for four days, after which a feast was held.

Discus   Javelin   Jumping   Running   Wrestling

GREAT BUDDHAS

Buddhism is one of the oldest religions in the world. It was founded in India in the 6th century B.C. by a teacher called Buddha, a name meaning "The Enlightened One." By the 3rd century B.C., Buddhism had become the main religion in Asia and today over 245 million people follow the Buddhist faith. Although originally an eastern religion, Buddhism is also practised in the West.

Buddhists believe that through meditation they can achieve a state of "Nirvana" or true spiritual knowledge, which will free them from physical and worldly suffering. The centre of Buddhist worship is the temple or shrine where there are always statues or carvings of Buddha. There are many thousands of images of Buddha throughout the Buddhist world, represented in a variety of ways.

The many faces of Buddha
We have chosen to illustrate Buddhist statues because they have a distinctive style and are quite unlike other religious statues. Here you can see three very different Buddhas.

The Shwethalyaung
One of the most extraordinary and life-like examples of Buddhist sculpture is the 10th century figure of Buddha in the city of Pegu in Burma. Known as the Shwethalyaung, the colossal statue is 55m (180ft) long and 16m (46ft) high at the shoulder. After Pegu was destroyed in 1757, the city was gradually overrun by the jungle. The Shwethalyaung lay hidden for centuries until it was discovered by chance in 1881. In 1906 it was enclosed in an iron pavilion and it was renovated in 1946.

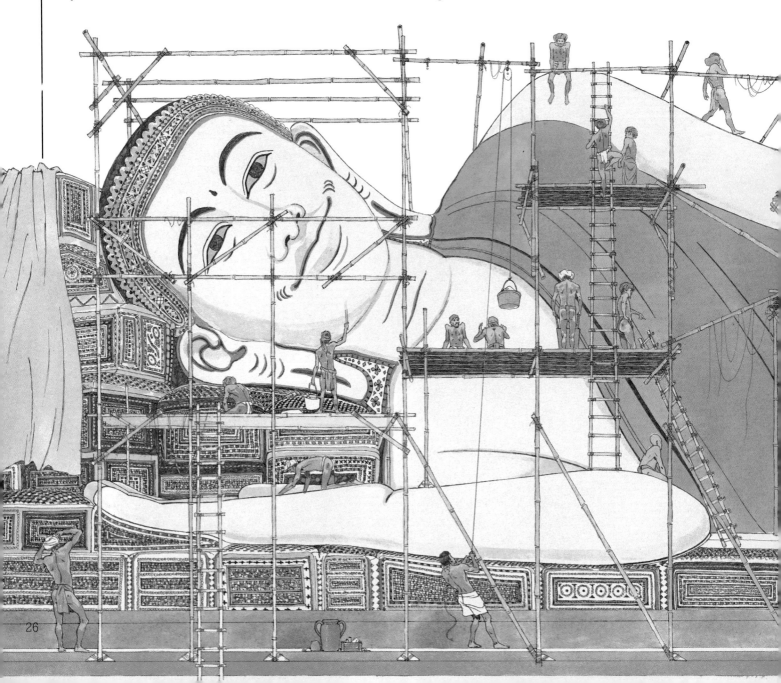

Wat Trimitr

Seated on a pedestal inside Wat Trimitr (Temple of the Golden Buddha) in Thailand, is a magnificent 5m (16ft) high figure of Buddha. It is made of 5.5 tons of solid gold and is one of the most valuable statues in the world. In order to conceal its priceless value, the 13th century statue was covered in a layer of plaster. Left in this state until 1953, its true nature was only revealed when the statue was dropped and the plaster cracked.

Gal Vihara Temple

In a secluded spot in the forest near Polonnaruva in Sri Lanka, lies the Gal Vihara Temple containing four splendid statues of Buddha, carved out of a single granite wall. They date from about the 12th century, and are depicted in different poses: two are seated, one is lying down and another is standing.

27

PLACES OF PILGRIMAGE

A pilgrimage is a journey to a holy place or sanctuary. Since ancient times, people have made long and perilous journeys in order to pay homage to a god or hero at a special shrine. Such places have a religious significance for various reasons. For instance, they might be the birthplace of a prophet, the final resting place of a saint, or, perhaps, even the site of a miracle.

All the major religions of the world have places that hold a special significance for their followers. Roman Catholic Christians go to Rome and Lourdes, Jews to Jerusalem, and Moslems to Mecca. These and many other sites across the world attract millions of pilgrims who go to worship their god and affirm their beliefs. Special services and religious rites are held, often taking place on holy days.

Many of the pilgrims who come to such places travel great distances, some making the journey for the one and only time in their lives. They come in search of spiritual guidance or healing.

Jerusalem

The golden city of Jerusalem, centre of the Jewish faith, attracts thousands of pilgrims each year. One of its most sacred shrines is the Wailing Wall. Said to be the only remaining part of the biblical Temple of Solomon, the Wall measures 50m (160ft) long and 18m (58ft) high. Jews from all over the world visit the shrine to mourn the destruction of the Temple and pray for its restoration. European travellers invented the term "Wailing Wall" when they saw how deeply it moved the emotions of all those who came to worship beside it.

Even the wall is believed to mourn. When dewdrops appear on its stones, it is said that they weep for the fall of the Temple.

Mecca

The city of Mecca in Saudi Arabia is the birthplace of the prophet Mohammed, the founder of Islam. As the principal city of the Islamic faith, it has become one of the most famous places of pilgrimage.

The Great Mosque

Founded by Mohammed in 630 A.D., the Great Mosque has a huge open courtyard that measures 164 × 111m (540 × 365ft) and is enclosed by several rows of decorative columns. Overlooking the courtyard, are seven minarets from which the "muezzins" summon the faithful to prayer.

Annual pilgrimage

According to Islamic tradition, all Moslems should make the pilgrimage to Mecca at least once in their lifetime. Each year over a million pilgrims make the journey to Mecca in the last month of the Moslem calendar. During this period, only Moslems are permitted to enter the Holy City.

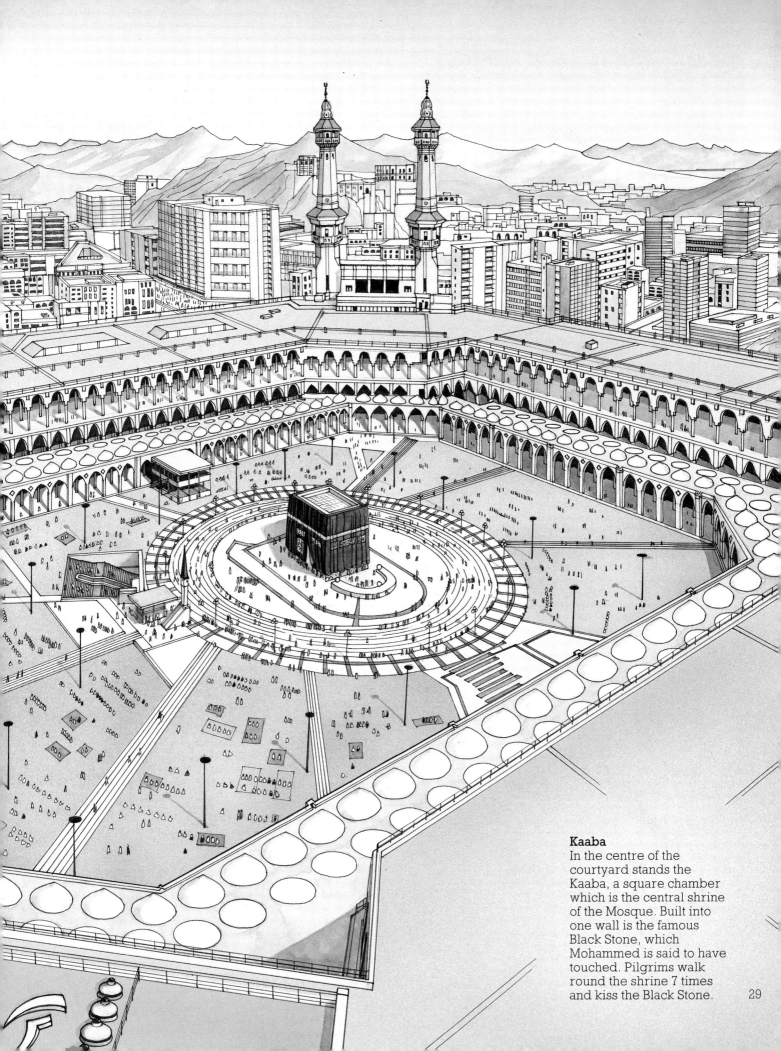

Kaaba
In the centre of the courtyard stands the Kaaba, a square chamber which is the central shrine of the Mosque. Built into one wall is the famous Black Stone, which Mohammed is said to have touched. Pilgrims walk round the shrine 7 times and kiss the Black Stone.

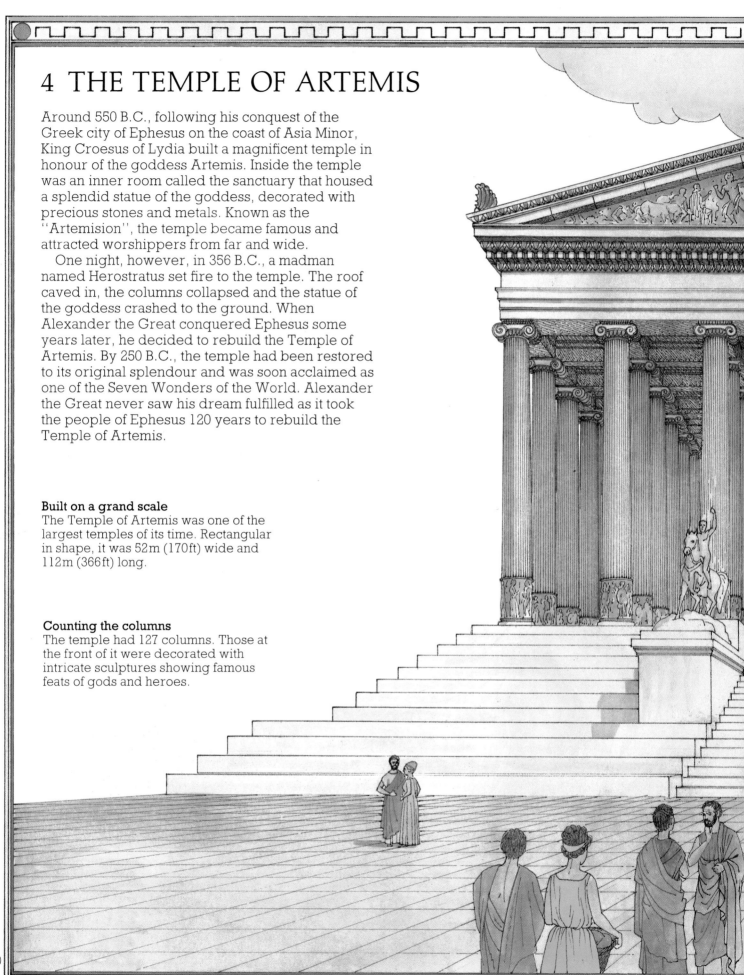

4 THE TEMPLE OF ARTEMIS

Around 550 B.C., following his conquest of the Greek city of Ephesus on the coast of Asia Minor, King Croesus of Lydia built a magnificent temple in honour of the goddess Artemis. Inside the temple was an inner room called the sanctuary that housed a splendid statue of the goddess, decorated with precious stones and metals. Known as the "Artemision", the temple became famous and attracted worshippers from far and wide.

One night, however, in 356 B.C., a madman named Herostratus set fire to the temple. The roof caved in, the columns collapsed and the statue of the goddess crashed to the ground. When Alexander the Great conquered Ephesus some years later, he decided to rebuild the Temple of Artemis. By 250 B.C., the temple had been restored to its original splendour and was soon acclaimed as one of the Seven Wonders of the World. Alexander the Great never saw his dream fulfilled as it took the people of Ephesus 120 years to rebuild the Temple of Artemis.

Built on a grand scale
The Temple of Artemis was one of the largest temples of its time. Rectangular in shape, it was 52m (170ft) wide and 112m (366ft) long.

Counting the columns
The temple had 127 columns. Those at the front of it were decorated with intricate sculptures showing famous feats of gods and heroes.

Mighty splendour
Here you can see what the temple looked like at the height of its glory, 2,000 years ago. It was famous not only for its size, but also for its magnificent sculptures.

BUILDING THE TEMPLE

The basic plan of the temple consisted of the main chamber and a porch at the front. Two rows of massive columns, 20m (65ft) tall and 3m (10ft) across, ran parallel to the walls of the temple. After the foundations had been laid and the temple platform built, the columns were slowly raised, block by block. Cranes and pulleys were used to lift the massive blocks of stone and scaffolding was put up around the temple as it took shape.

The building was made of limestone faced with marble, apart from the columns which were built entirely of marble. The last part of the temple to be built was the roof, after which the sculptors set to work on the elaborate decorations that made the temple famous.

Taking shape

In this picture you can see how the Temple of Artemis was actually built. Large cranes and strong ropes are being used to hoist sections of the columns into position.

Forming a picture

Many people have tried to work out what the temple looked like. Pictures found on coins of that period have helped to give us a good idea.

Two against one

Most Greek temples had only one row of columns but the Temple of Artemis, one of the grandest buildings of its time, was one of the few exceptions.

Where the temple was

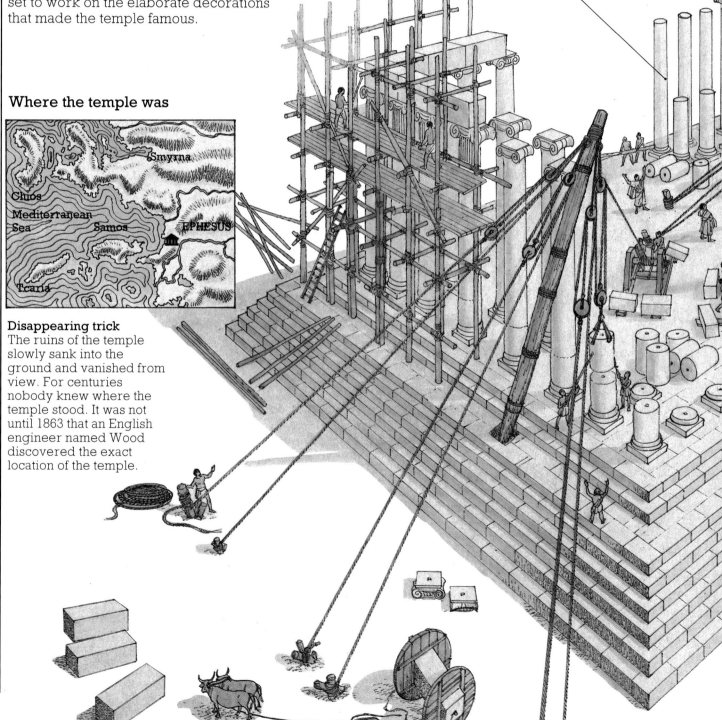

Smyrna
Chios
Mediterranean Sea
Samos
EPHESUS
Icaria

Disappearing trick

The ruins of the temple slowly sank into the ground and vanished from view. For centuries nobody knew where the temple stood. It was not until 1863 that an English engineer named Wood discovered the exact location of the temple.

32

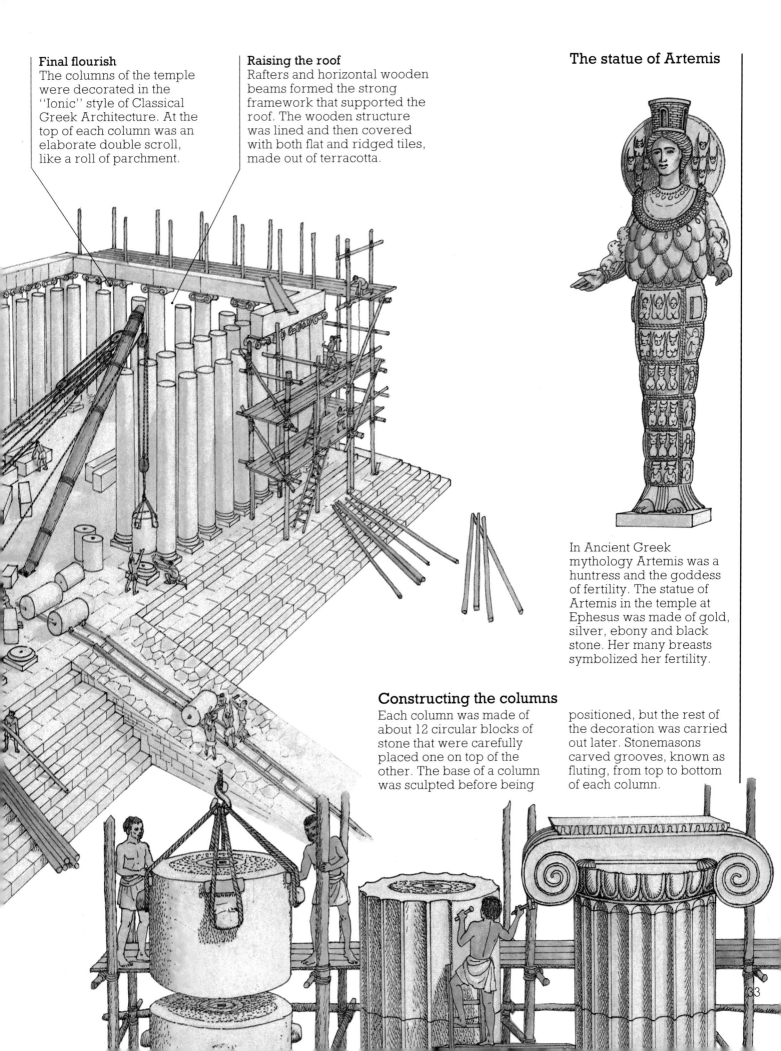

Final flourish

The columns of the temple were decorated in the "Ionic" style of Classical Greek Architecture. At the top of each column was an elaborate double scroll, like a roll of parchment.

Raising the roof

Rafters and horizontal wooden beams formed the strong framework that supported the roof. The wooden structure was lined and then covered with both flat and ridged tiles, made out of terracotta.

The statue of Artemis

In Ancient Greek mythology Artemis was a huntress and the goddess of fertility. The statue of Artemis in the temple at Ephesus was made of gold, silver, ebony and black stone. Her many breasts symbolized her fertility.

Constructing the columns

Each column was made of about 12 circular blocks of stone that were carefully placed one on top of the other. The base of a column was sculpted before being positioned, but the rest of the decoration was carried out later. Stonemasons carved grooves, known as fluting, from top to bottom of each column.

33

REACHING FOR THE HEAVENS

Temples, such as the Temple of Artemis, have been built since the earliest times in many parts of the world. The first churches ever built only date back to the A.D. 300s, but many churches and cathedrals now rank amongst the most magnificent and ornate buildings ever created.

Often intended by their builders to present an image of heaven to worshippers, many churches are large and richly decorated. Even in the poorest countries, the wealth and power of the Church have ensured that little expense was spared when it came to building churches and cathedrals. Varying enormously in style, depending on the time and place in which they were built, churches are often so grand that they dominate the skyline of their town or city. Some have soaring spires and others magnificent domes. All, however, were built with the same goal: to be houses of godly worship.

Four contrasting churches
The four churches pictured here are in different countries and are all very different in character and style. Each one is extraordinary in its own right: either because of its size or dimensions or because of its total originality.

Cathedral of the Sagrada Família (Holy Family)
Antonio Gaudi worked on his cathedral from 1883 until his death in 1926, but it has never been finished. Its ornate spires soar above Barcelona but it would take until the 22nd century to complete the rest of the cathedral.

St. Basil's Cathedral, Moscow
Its brilliantly coloured onion-shaped domes and belfries give St. Basil's, in Red Square, Moscow, a fairy-tale appearance. Built from 1555 to 1560, on the orders of Ivan the Terrible, it is really nine churches – a central chapel surrounded by eight smaller ones. The cathedral is now a museum.

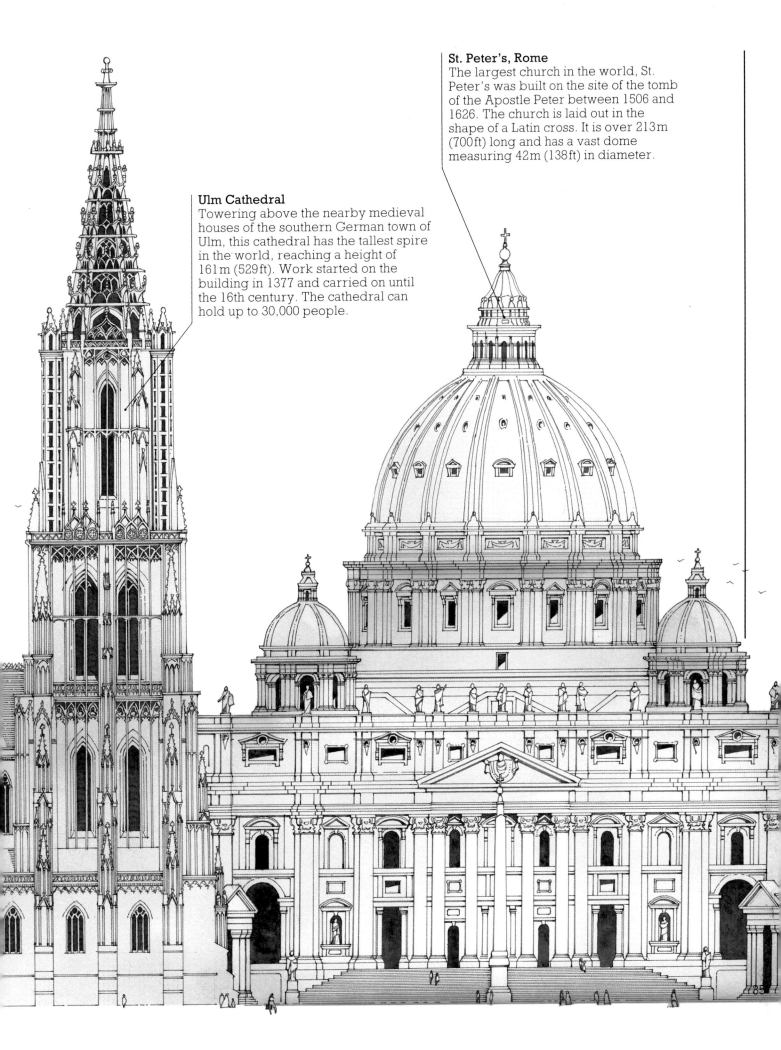

St. Peter's, Rome
The largest church in the world, St. Peter's was built on the site of the tomb of the Apostle Peter between 1506 and 1626. The church is laid out in the shape of a Latin cross. It is over 213m (700ft) long and has a vast dome measuring 42m (138ft) in diameter.

Ulm Cathedral
Towering above the nearby medieval houses of the southern German town of Ulm, this cathedral has the tallest spire in the world, reaching a height of 161m (529ft). Work started on the building in 1377 and carried on until the 16th century. The cathedral can hold up to 30,000 people.

BUILDING A CATHEDRAL

The most magnificent of all the churches, cathedrals are masterpieces of craftsmanship and often took hundreds of years to complete. The Middle Ages were the golden period of cathedral building in Europe and many new cathedrals were built in what is called the Gothic style. They have soaring, pointed arches, high ceilings with crisscross stone ribs and walls with large wing-like supports that are called buttresses.

The first Gothic cathedrals were built in northern France, and perhaps the most typical of these is the cathedral at Chartres, southwest of Paris, which has survived almost without change from the early 13th century to the present day.

The finishing touches
Rebuilt in the Gothic style between 1194 and 1260 A.D., Chartres is famous for its stained glass windows and its sculptures. Here you can see the final stages of its construction in progress.

High above the ground
Wooden frames for the roof were made on the ground, then hoisted up to the top of the walls. Scaffolding was put up and stones for the roof were lifted up by a windlass.

Soaring walls
The walls were built of tall piers made of cut stone. The spaces between them were mostly filled with the ornamental stone tracery or framework for the windows, and partly with solid wall.

Strengthening the walls
To help the walls take the weight of the ceiling, stone buttresses, or supports were built. They were connected to the outer side of the walls by arches called flying buttresses.

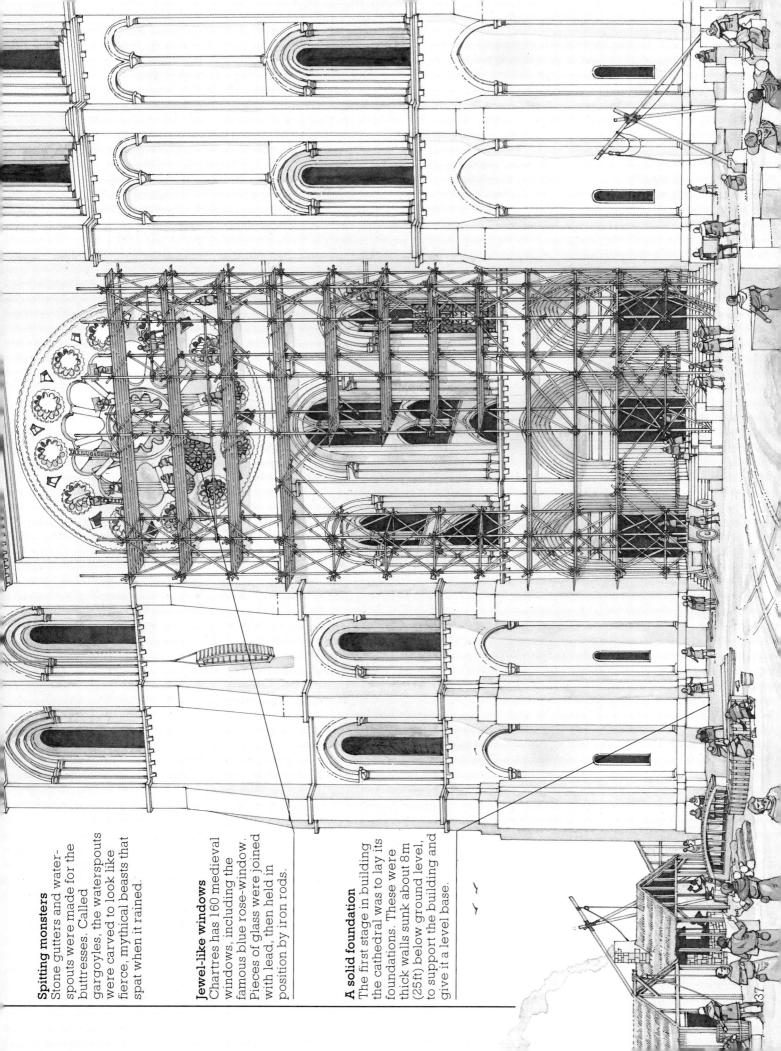

Spitting monsters
Stone gutters and water-
spouts were made for the
buttresses. Called
gargoyles, the waterspouts
were carved to look like
fierce, mythical beasts that
spat when it rained.

Jewel-like windows
Chartres has 160 medieval
windows, including the
famous blue rose-window.
Pieces of glass were joined
with lead, then held in
position by iron rods.

A solid foundation
The first stage in building
the cathedral was to lay its
foundations. These were
thick walls sunk about 8m
(25ft) below ground level,
to support the building and
give it a level base.

37

5 THE MAUSOLEUM AT HALICARNASSUS

King Mausolus ruled over Caria, part of modern-day Turkey, in the 4th century B.C.. He was an ambitious king and attacked many nearby cities and states. With the money from his conquests, he built a new capital city at Halicarnassus.

Towards the end of his life, King Mausolus decided to build himself a tomb, as a monument to his power. He wanted it to be the most magnificent tomb ever seen. No expense was spared and the finished tomb was so grand that it was named a mausoleum, after Mausolus.

The end of the mausoleum

The mausoleum survived for centuries, but eventually fell into ruin. In 1581, stones were taken from the ruins and used to build a fortress.

A mighty size

The base of the mausoleum covered an area measuring 38.4m by 32m (126ft by 105ft). The finished tomb was over 42.6m (140ft) tall.

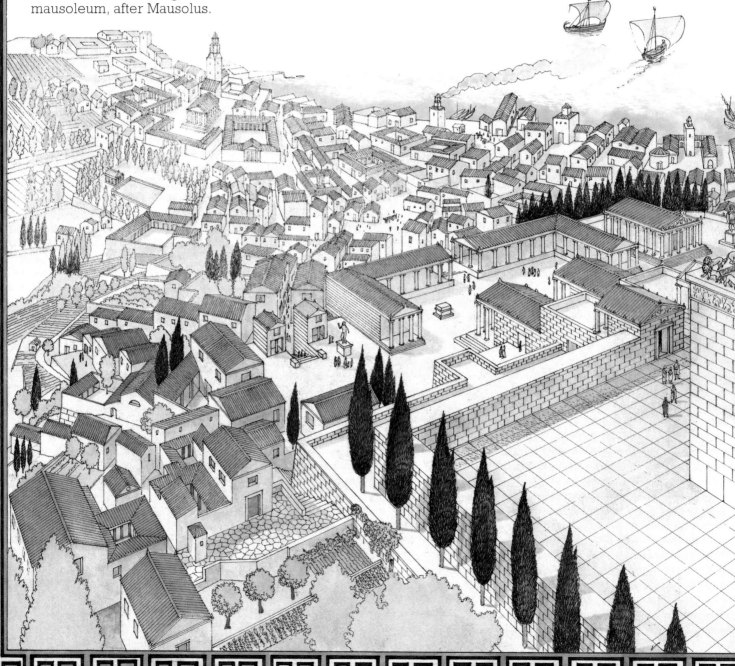

A lofty temple
Archaeologists have worked out that the mausoleum must have looked rather like a Classical Greek temple on top of an enormous plinth.

BUILDING THE MAUSOLEUM

Mausolus wanted the mausoleum to be ready in time for his death. But when he did die, in 353 B.C., the building was still incomplete. It was only finished four years later by his widow, Artemisia.

The mausoleum was designed to be at once both a temple and a tomb. It was built of gleaming white marble, and consisted of three tiers, on top of which stood a temple surrounded by columns and statues. There was a pyramid-like roof on top of the temple and at its summit stood an enormous statue of Mausolus and Artemisia standing proudly in a horse-drawn chariot.

A towering achievement

According to ancient manuscripts, the mausoleum was built in four stages using a workforce of many thousands of men. Work continued on the site for over ten years.

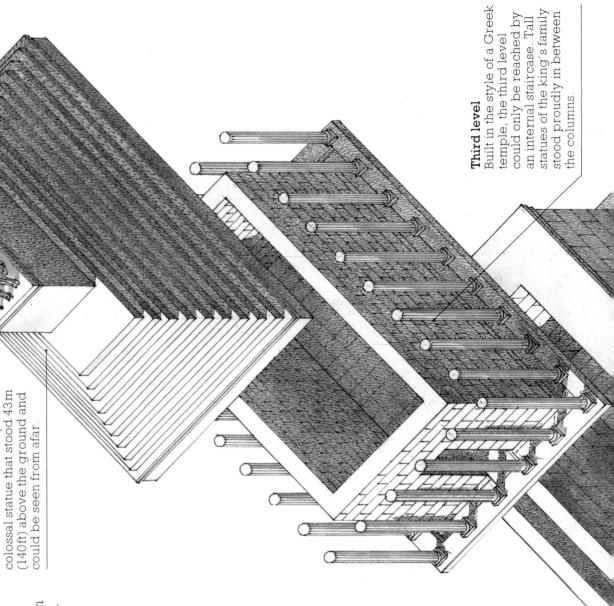

Top level
Supported by the columns of the temple was a pyramid-like roof. It was crowned by a colossal statue that stood 43m (140ft) above the ground and could be seen from afar.

Third level
Built in the style of a Greek temple, the third level could only be reached by an internal staircase. Tall statues of the king's family stood proudly in between the columns.

The builders

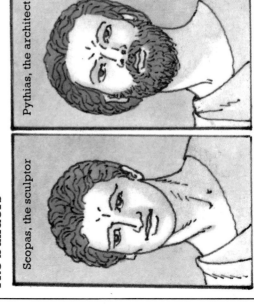

Scopas, the sculptor   Pythias, the architect

When Mausolus died, Artemisia summoned the best architects and sculptors to Halicarnassus to finish the tomb. Pythias, a Greek architect, supervised the construction and Scopas, a Greek sculptor, was in charge of the sculpted decorations and friezes.

Second level

Carved around the outside of the second section was a row of lions that guarded the tomb. Adorning the walls were sculpted decorations showing fierce battles between Greeks and the legendary female warriors, the Amazons.

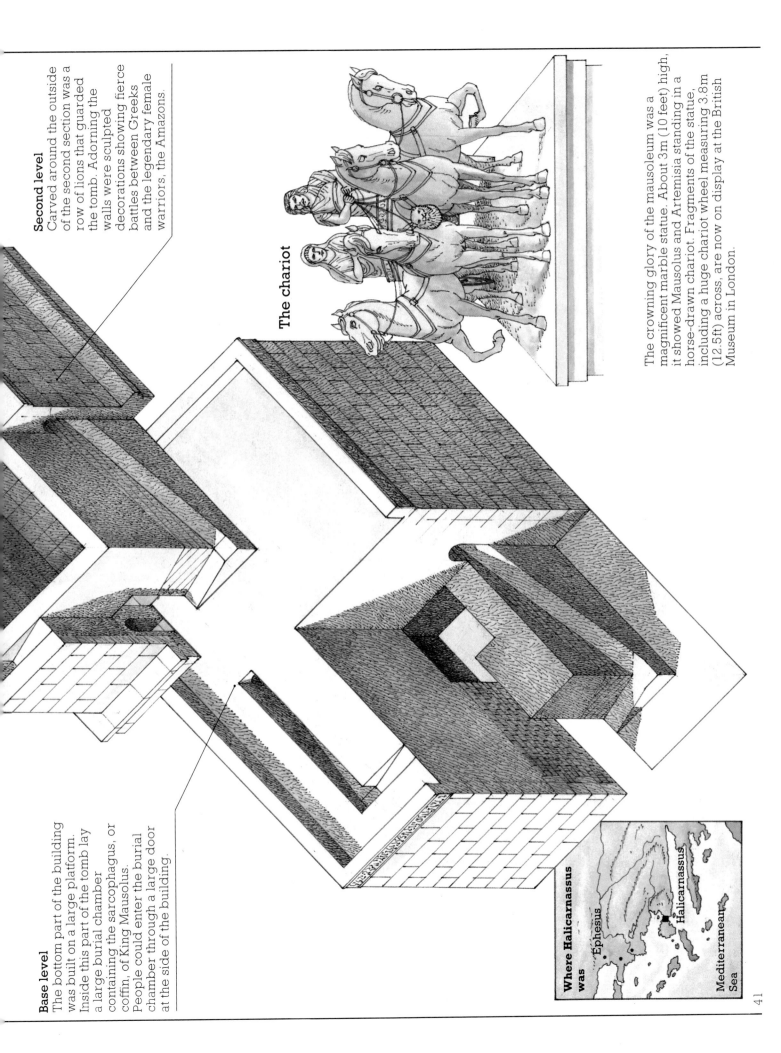

The chariot

The crowning glory of the mausoleum was a magnificent marble statue. About 3m (10 feet) high, it showed Mausolus and Artemisia standing in a horse-drawn chariot. Fragments of the statue, including a huge chariot wheel measuring 3.8m (12.5ft) across, are now on display at the British Museum in London.

Base level

The bottom part of the building was built on a large platform. Inside this part of the tomb lay a large burial chamber containing the sarcophagus, or coffin, of King Mausolus. People could enter the burial chamber through a large door at the side of the building.

Where Halicarnassus was

Ephesus

Halicarnassus

Mediterranean Sea

THE TAJ MAHAL

Standing on the banks of the Jumna River, near Agra in northern India, is the Taj Mahal, one of the world's most beautiful and romantic tombs. Shah Jahan, one of the Mogul emperors of India in the 17th century, built the tomb in memory of his favourite wife, Mumtaz-i-Mahal, who died in childbirth. The heartbroken Shah planned to build a copy of the Taj in black marble on the other side of the river as his own tomb. Before he could embark on his second masterpiece, however, his son seized power and imprisoned him. Shah Jahan spent the rest of his days in the fort at Agra, looking along the muddy river to the final resting place of his wife. Shah himself died in 1658 and was buried alongside his wife in her tomb.

An "otherworldly" monument
With its onion-shaped dome and slender minarets or towers, the Taj Mahal has a fairy tale quality. The white marble of the monument changes colour according to the weather and time of day.

A peaceful approach
The approach to the monument leads first through a gateway, then through a beautiful walled garden where a watercourse flanked by cypress trees reflects the marble tomb.

A labour of love
Begun in 1632, it took 20,000 men 22 years to build the Taj Mahal. They included craftsmen from all over Central Asia and European experts, from France and Italy.

42

All shapes and sizes

Since the earliest times, people have built tombs and monuments to honour the dead. Constructed in a wide variety of styles, each one is grand in its own way.

The Lincoln Memorial

Built in honour of Abraham Lincoln, this memorial in Washington D.C. is built of white marble and looks like a Greek temple.

Tomb of Theodoric the Goth

This tomb was built at Ravenna in Italy as early as A.D. 530. Its dome-shaped roof was hewn out of stone.

Gunbad-i-Qabus of Gungan

Built in the early 11th century in Persia, this rocket-shaped tomb is built entirely of brick and stands 50m (70ft) high.

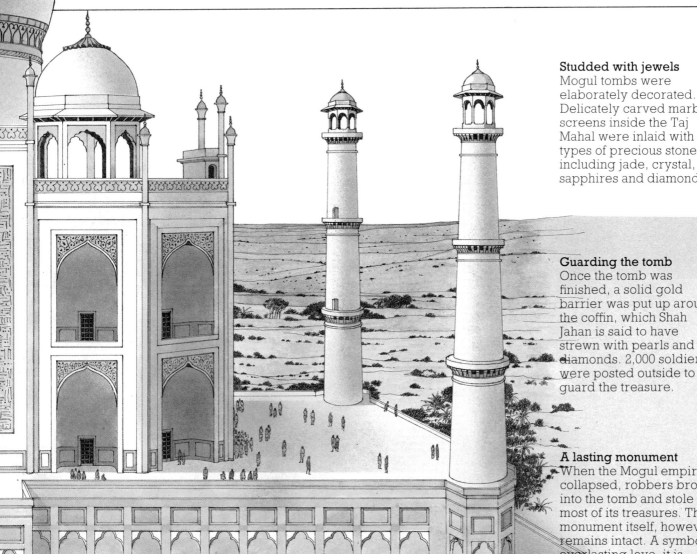

Studded with jewels

Mogul tombs were elaborately decorated. Delicately carved marble screens inside the Taj Mahal were inlaid with 43 types of precious stone, including jade, crystal, sapphires and diamonds.

Guarding the tomb

Once the tomb was finished, a solid gold barrier was put up around the coffin, which Shah Jahan is said to have strewn with pearls and diamonds. 2,000 soldiers were posted outside to guard the treasure.

A lasting monument

When the Mogul empire collapsed, robbers broke into the tomb and stole most of its treasures. The monument itself, however, remains intact. A symbol of everlasting love, it is India's most famous sight.

43

GUARDIANS OF THE TOMBS

As far back as the 10th century B.C., Chinese emperors built themselves magnificent tombs on the outskirts of their capital cities. These tombs were filled with royal treasures, but it was another feature that made them unique: both the tombs and the roads that led to them were guarded by massive statues of animals and warriors.

These statues were supposed to guard the soul of the emperor as his body was taken to the tomb, to ward off evil spirits, to bring good luck and to serve the emperor in the next world.

Here you can find out about the guardians of the tomb of the first Emperor of China and those of the Ming tombs, built nearly 2,000 years later.

The terracotta army
In 1974, peasants digging a well near the city of Xi'an, in north west China, came across thousands of life-size terracotta warriors that had been standing guard by the tomb of Emperor Qui Shi Huang for over 2,000 years.

China's first emperor
Work began on the tomb of Qui Shi Huang (259–209 B.C.) when he came to the throne and continued in secrecy for 36 years. The tomb was built as an underground "imperial city", with a throne room and treasure houses.

The undiscovered tomb
Archaeologists have not yet excavated the tomb, but in three underground vaults, 2 km (1 mile) from the tomb, the terracotta army was found – 8,000 statues of soldiers, some with horses and chariots, grouped in battle order.

True to life
Made of pottery, the figures are about 1.8m (6ft) tall on average and are hollow, with solid arms and legs. The heads and hands were modelled separately. Each figure has different features and expressions and wears marks of rank.

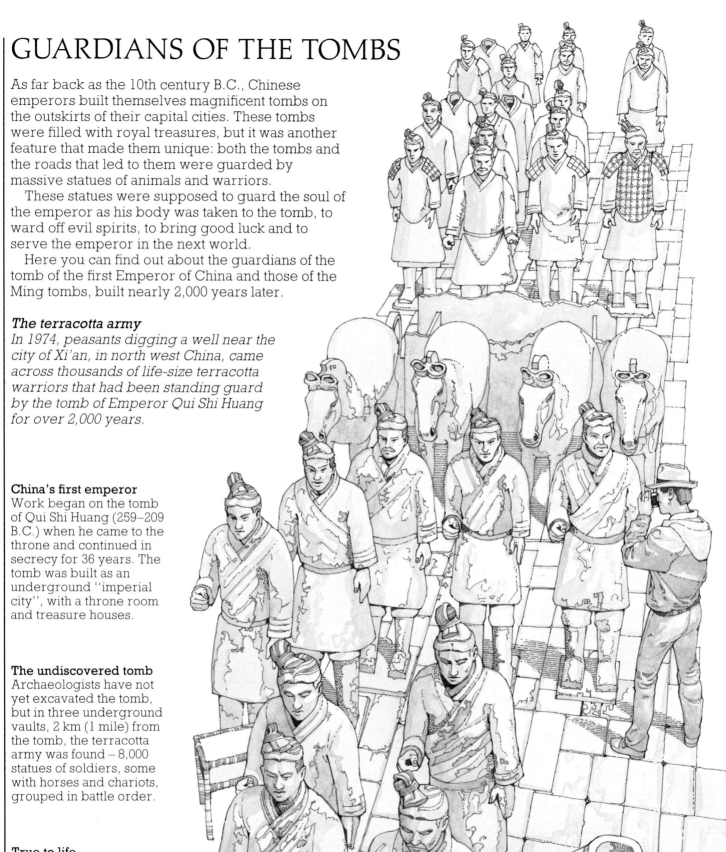

The Spirit Way to the Ming Tombs

30 miles to the north of Peking are the tombs of the emperors of the Ming dynasty, who ruled China from the 15th to the 17th centuries A.D.. The Spirit Way was the road along which an emperor's coffin was taken to the tombs. 7km (4 miles) long, it represented the journey taken by the emperor's soul from life to a peaceful death. The Spirit Way passes through several gateways and arches, before coming to the Avenue of Animals.

The Avenue of Animals

Lining the Avenue of Animals are massive statues of animals, up to 3.5m (12ft) tall, each made from a single block of blue limestone. There are 24 pairs of animals in all, facing each other in pairs on either side of the road: lions, camels, horses, elephants and mythical beasts.

Giant figures

After passing through the animals, the Spirit Way comes to 12 colossal statues of Chinese officials called mandarins. Some represent the emperor's personal soldiers. Dressed in long coats of armour and close-fitting helmets, they carry swords or batons and look very fierce.

45

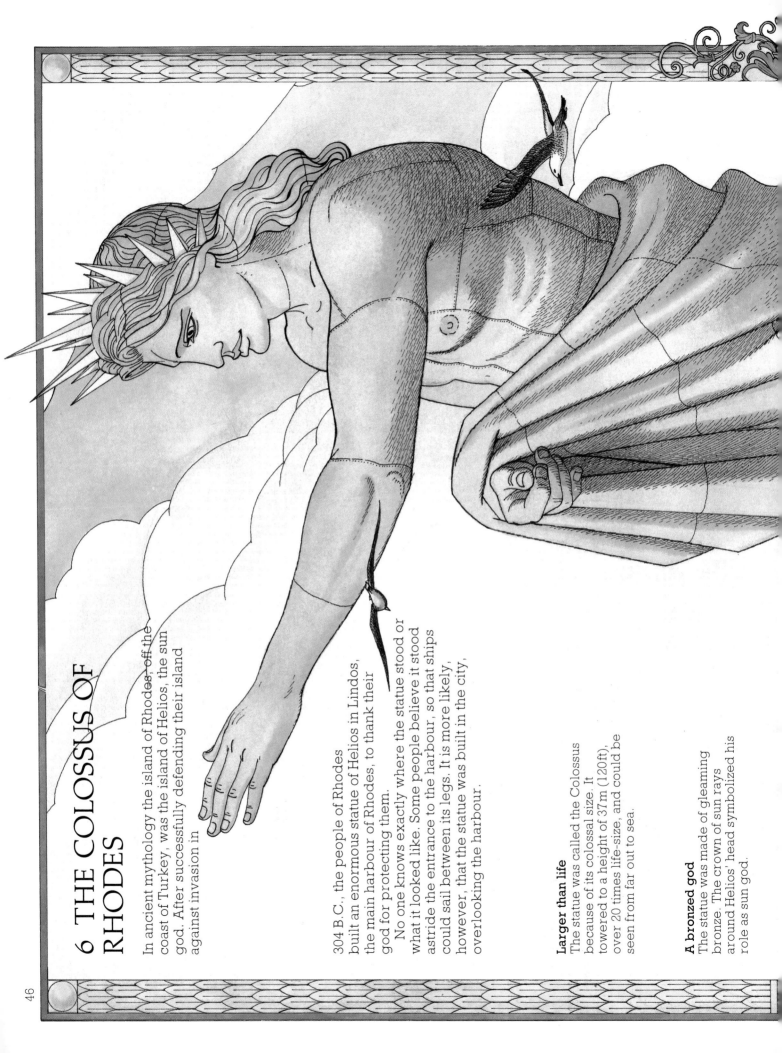

6 THE COLOSSUS OF RHODES

In ancient mythology the island of Rhodes, off the coast of Turkey, was the island of Helios, the sun god. After successfully defending their island against invasion in

304 B.C., the people of Rhodes built an enormous statue of Helios in Lindos, the main harbour of Rhodes, to thank their god for protecting them.

No one knows exactly where the statue stood or what it looked like. Some people believe it stood astride the entrance to the harbour, so that ships could sail between its legs. It is more likely, however, that the statue was built in the city, overlooking the harbour.

Larger than life

The statue was called the Colossus because of its colossal size. It towered to a height of 37m (120ft), over 20 times life-size, and could be seen from far out to sea.

A bronzed god

The statue was made of gleaming bronze. The crown of sun rays around Helios' head symbolized his role as sun god.

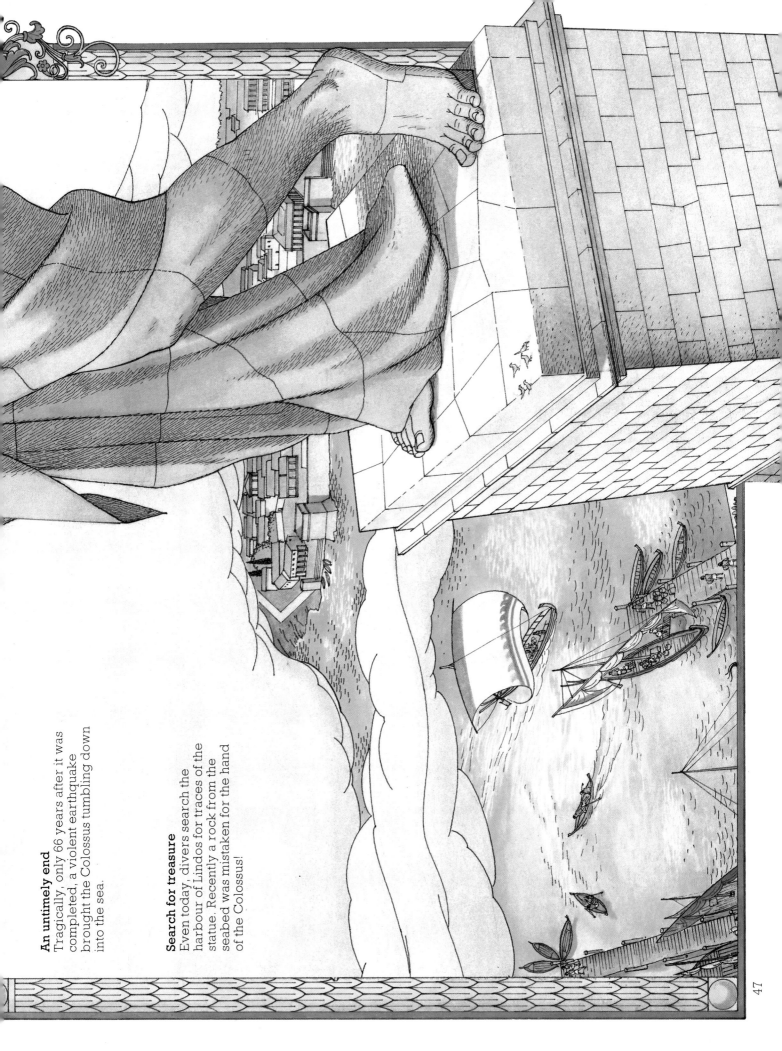

An untimely end

Tragically, only 66 years after it was completed, a violent earthquake brought the Colossus tumbling down into the sea.

Search for treasure

Even today, divers search the harbour of Lindos for traces of the statue. Recently a rock from the seabed was mistaken for the hand of the Colossus!

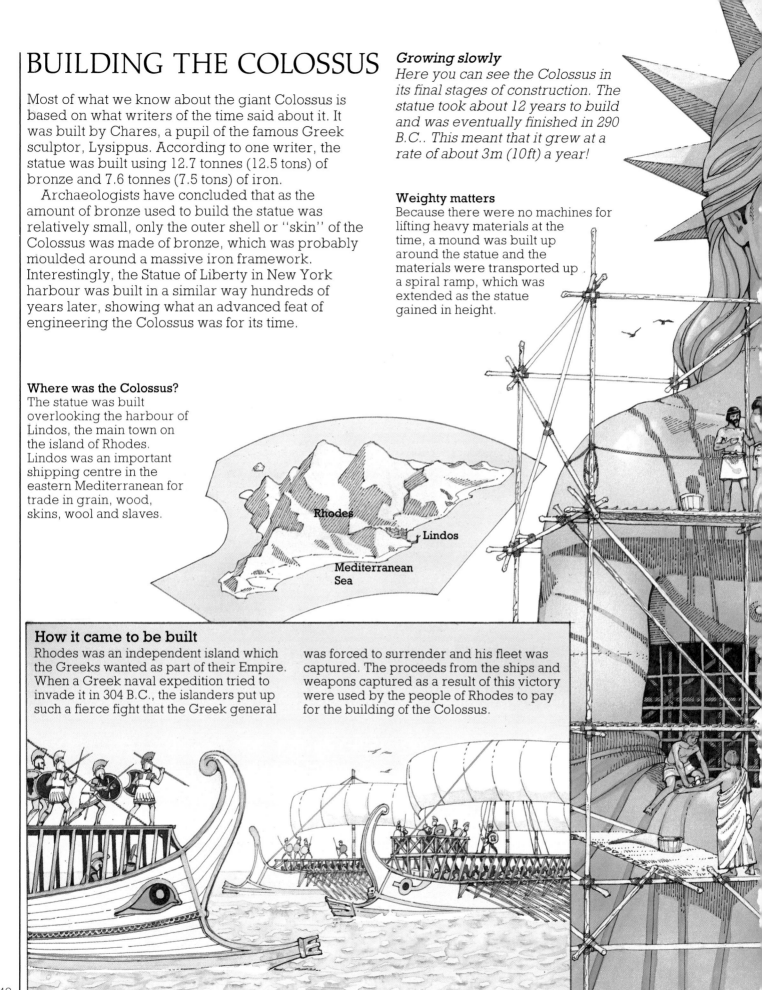

BUILDING THE COLOSSUS

Most of what we know about the giant Colossus is based on what writers of the time said about it. It was built by Chares, a pupil of the famous Greek sculptor, Lysippus. According to one writer, the statue was built using 12.7 tonnes (12.5 tons) of bronze and 7.6 tonnes (7.5 tons) of iron.

Archaeologists have concluded that as the amount of bronze used to build the statue was relatively small, only the outer shell or "skin" of the Colossus was made of bronze, which was probably moulded around a massive iron framework. Interestingly, the Statue of Liberty in New York harbour was built in a similar way hundreds of years later, showing what an advanced feat of engineering the Colossus was for its time.

Where was the Colossus?
The statue was built overlooking the harbour of Lindos, the main town on the island of Rhodes. Lindos was an important shipping centre in the eastern Mediterranean for trade in grain, wood, skins, wool and slaves.

Rhodes

Lindos

Mediterranean Sea

Growing slowly
Here you can see the Colossus in its final stages of construction. The statue took about 12 years to build and was eventually finished in 290 B.C.. This meant that it grew at a rate of about 3m (10ft) a year!

Weighty matters
Because there were no machines for lifting heavy materials at the time, a mound was built up around the statue and the materials were transported up a spiral ramp, which was extended as the statue gained in height.

How it came to be built
Rhodes was an independent island which the Greeks wanted as part of their Empire. When a Greek naval expedition tried to invade it in 304 B.C., the islanders put up such a fierce fight that the Greek general was forced to surrender and his fleet was captured. The proceeds from the ships and weapons captured as a result of this victory were used by the people of Rhodes to pay for the building of the Colossus.

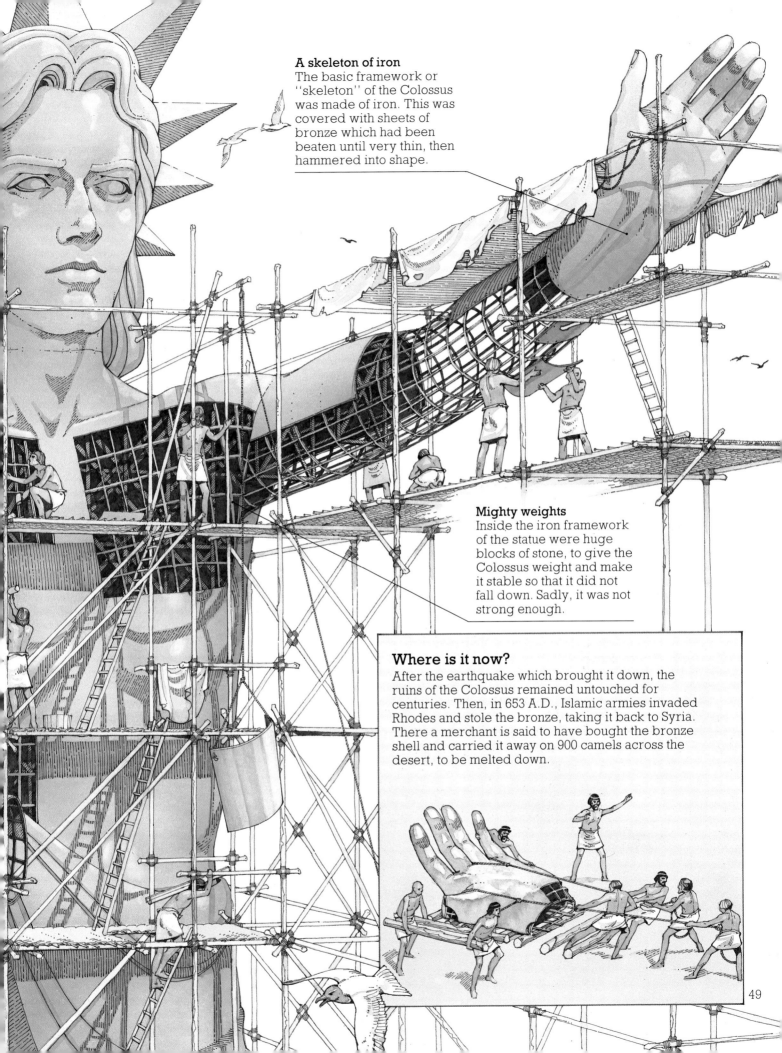

A skeleton of iron
The basic framework or "skeleton" of the Colossus was made of iron. This was covered with sheets of bronze which had been beaten until very thin, then hammered into shape.

Mighty weights
Inside the iron framework of the statue were huge blocks of stone, to give the Colossus weight and make it stable so that it did not fall down. Sadly, it was not strong enough.

Where is it now?
After the earthquake which brought it down, the ruins of the Colossus remained untouched for centuries. Then, in 653 A.D., Islamic armies invaded Rhodes and stole the bronze, taking it back to Syria. There a merchant is said to have bought the bronze shell and carried it away on 900 camels across the desert, to be melted down.

49

THE LIGHT OF LIBERTY

The Statue of Liberty in New York was built by a French sculptor, Auguste Bartholdi, and was originally called "Liberty Enlightening the World". One of the largest statues ever built, it was presented by the people of France to the United States in 1884 to commemorate the centenary of the American Declaration of Independence. The statue was built in Paris and later reassembled in New York.

The torch bearer
Liberty is carrying the torch of freedom in her right hand and stepping out of broken chains. In her left hand she holds a tablet with the inscription "July 4 1776" – American Independence Day.

Torch
The torch towers 93m (305ft) above the base of the pedestal and was recently replaced. At night it is brightly lit by powerful mercury lamps.

Crown
Visitors are allowed as high as the crown. Here, just above Liberty's nose, which is as long as you are tall, there is an observation platform providing a magnificent view of the New York skyline.

Where it is
The statue stands on Liberty Island, at the entrance to New York Harbour.

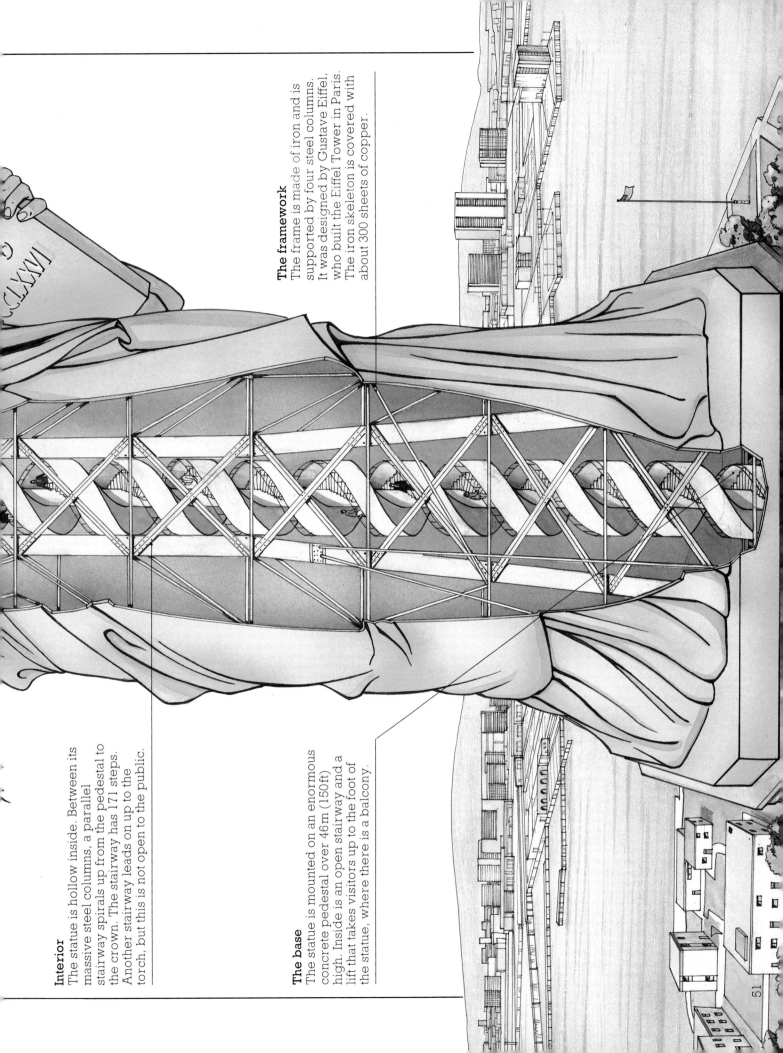

Interior
The statue is hollow inside. Between its massive steel columns, a parallel stairway spirals up from the pedestal to the crown. The stairway has 171 steps. Another stairway leads on up to the torch, but this is not open to the public.

The base
The statue is mounted on an enormous concrete pedestal over 46m (150ft) high. Inside is an open stairway and a lift that takes visitors up to the foot of the statue, where there is a balcony.

The framework
The frame is made of iron and is supported by four steel columns. It was designed by Gustave Eiffel, who built the Eiffel Tower in Paris. The iron skeleton is covered with about 300 sheets of copper.

51

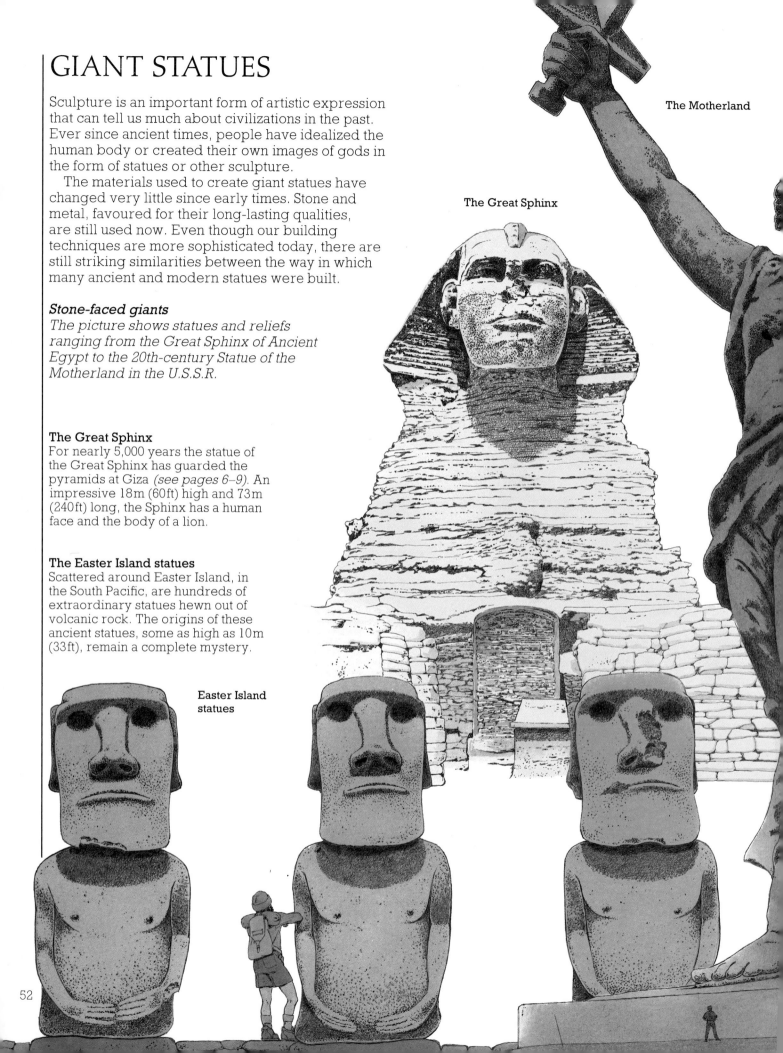

GIANT STATUES

Sculpture is an important form of artistic expression that can tell us much about civilizations in the past. Ever since ancient times, people have idealized the human body or created their own images of gods in the form of statues or other sculpture.

The materials used to create giant statues have changed very little since early times. Stone and metal, favoured for their long-lasting qualities, are still used now. Even though our building techniques are more sophisticated today, there are still striking similarities between the way in which many ancient and modern statues were built.

Stone-faced giants
The picture shows statues and reliefs ranging from the Great Sphinx of Ancient Egypt to the 20th-century Statue of the Motherland in the U.S.S.R.

The Great Sphinx
For nearly 5,000 years the statue of the Great Sphinx has guarded the pyramids at Giza *(see pages 6–9)*. An impressive 18m (60ft) high and 73m (240ft) long, the Sphinx has a human face and the body of a lion.

The Easter Island statues
Scattered around Easter Island, in the South Pacific, are hundreds of extraordinary statues hewn out of volcanic rock. The origins of these ancient statues, some as high as 10m (33ft), remain a complete mystery.

The Motherland

The Great Sphinx

Easter Island statues

The Motherland
On a hill top outside Volgograd in the U.S.S.R. stands the colossal concrete "Motherland" statue. It was designed in 1967 by the sculptor Yevgenyi Vuchetich, to commemorate the Battle of Stalingrad (1942–43). Measuring 82m (270ft), it is ranked as the tallest statue in the world.

The Corcovado Christ

The Corcovado Christ
Perched on Mount Corcovado in Rio de Janeiro, Brazil, stands a huge statue of Christ. The 40m (130ft) high concrete statue was designed by sculptor Paul Landowski, and completed within five years in 1931.

Mount Rushmore

Mount Rushmore
Out of the sheer granite cliff of Mount Rushmore , South Dakota, U.S.A., stare the faces of four American presidents. From 1927 to 1941, Gutzon Borglum used dynamite and pneumatic drills to create the likenesses of Washington, Jefferson, Lincoln and Roosevelt. Each head measures 18m (60ft) and can be seen from a distance of 96km (60 miles).

7 THE PHAROS OF ALEXANDRIA

In 279 B.C., after 20 years work, the lighthouse of Alexandria was completed and was immediately hailed as one of the Wonders of the World. It was the first large lighthouse ever constructed, and was so solidly built that it stood for over a thousand years, surviving several earthquakes.

The lighthouse took its name from the island of Pharos, on which it was built. In many languages the word "pharos" still means "lighthouse" today. The island was outside the harbour of Alexandria and was linked to the mainland by a causeway.

We have a good idea of what the lighthouse looked like from pictures on Roman coins and from descriptions of it by writers of the time. The Pharos rose to a height of about 122m (400ft) and could be seen by ships many miles out to sea.

A three-storey lighthouse

The Pharos was built of white marble, in three storeys that each tapered towards the top. The lower section was rectangular, the middle one octagonal and the top section cylindrical.

A long life

In 796 A.D. the lighthouse was badly damaged by an earthquake and later a fortress was built upon its ruins. The foundations of the ancient Pharos can still be seen where Quait Bay Fort stands today.

Shining bright

At the top of the lighthouse a fire was kept burning day and night. The light from it was so bright that it could be seen from as far away as 56km (35 miles) out to sea.

ALEXANDRIA

To many people the Pharos of Alexandria symbolized the power and glory of the Greek nation founded by Alexander the Great. Alexander founded many cities and they were all named Alexandria after him, but the greatest of them all was the city on the Mediterranean coast of Egypt where the Pharos and many other magnificent buildings were erected.

Under the rule of Ptolemy I, one of Alexander's generals, and his family, who ruled Egypt for 300 years, Alexandria became the centre of world trade and learning, and one of the most splendid cities in the ancient world.

A bird's-eye view
Here is the view a bird would have had of Alexandria as it flew over the Pharos towards the city. Many of the buildings in Alexandria were Classical Greek in style, with columns and statues.

Who built the Pharos?
Alexander the Great had the idea of building the lighthouse. Sostratus was the architect and builder. Ptolemy I ordered the work to begin and it was completed in the reign of Ptolemy II.

A centre of learning
Ptolemy I founded many buildings where scholars could study science. There were Botanical Gardens, an astronomical observatory and a school of anatomy with equipment for dissecting bodies.

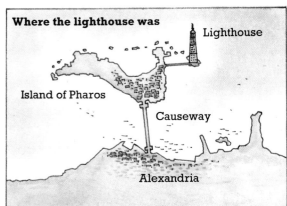

Where the lighthouse was

Lighthouse

Island of Pharos

Causeway

Alexandria

The Pharos
Crowning the very top of the lighthouse stood a statue of Helios, the Greek god of the sun.

A huge mirror
The fire at the top of the lighthouse was said to be "a pillar of fire by night, of smoke by day". The light of the fire was reflected out to sea by an enormous concave mirror.

Inner ramp
The upper part of the lighthouse was reached by a sloping, spiral ramp. Fuel for the fire was carried up it in horse-drawn carts, then hoisted to the top by pulleys.

Keeping watch
There were hundreds of rooms leading off the ramp. These had outward-facing windows and were used to keep watch out to sea and for experiments by astronomers.

Solid as a rock
A walled platform around the base of the lighthouse protected it from the sea. Drinking water, supplied from the mainland by an aqueduct, was stored in the base of the building.

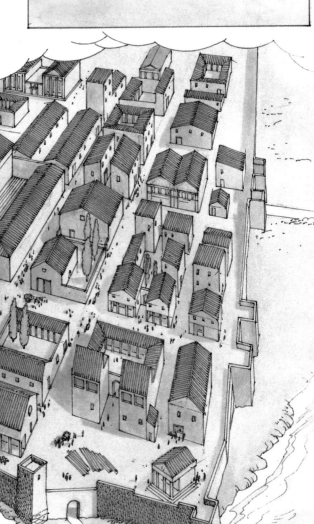

The first museum
Amongst the buildings Ptolemy founded were the Museum, the first of its kind, where mathematics and science were studied, and a magnificent library, which housed the largest collection of books in the ancient world.

57

TOWERING CONSTRUCTIONS

Despite their very different appearances, the Eiffel Tower in Paris and the Empire State Building in New York are remarkably similar in construction. Both have simple skeleton frames – the Eiffel Tower's is made of wrought iron, the Empire State's of steel – with thousands of cross braces to hold the structure rigid. This simple but effective system ensures that despite their great height, neither building sways much in the wind.

The only significant difference between the two is that the Empire State Building has lightweight exterior walls enclosing the building and attached to the central frame. This method of building was first used in the late 19th century when buildings were first constructed around iron frames. It allowed architects to design higher and higher skyscrapers, as they no longer had to construct a building with thick exterior walls to support the height.

Under construction

Slowly but surely the Eiffel Tower and the Empire State Building rise up to completion. Both were built of prefabricated sections that were hoisted into position by large cranes.

The Eiffel Tower

Erected between 1887 and 1889 in time for the exhibition celebrating the centenary of the French Revolution, the Eiffel Tower served as the entrance archway to the exhibition site. The tower was named after its designer, the French engineer and bridge builder, Alexandre Gustave Eiffel. 300m (986ft) tall, it has over 15,000 different parts, is held together with over 2.5 million rivets, and weighs 8,564,816kg (9,441 tons).

The Empire State Building

Designed by the American architectural firm of Shreve, Lamb and Harrison, the Empire State Building was constructed in 1930. It took only eight months to build, rising at the rate of 4.5 storeys a day to a total height of 381m (1,250ft) above the streets of New York. More than 3,400 people built its 102 storeys, using 61 million kg (60,000 tons) of steel for the frame, 740,000kg (730 tons) of aluminium and stainless steel for the outer walls, and 10 million bricks and 5,600 cubic metres of stone (200,000 cubic feet) for the lower floors and walls. The building contains 7,600km (4,730 miles) of electrical wire, 112km (70 miles) of water pipe, 80km (50 miles) of radiator pipe, and 6,500 windows. The total cost, including the cost of the site, was $40 million (£25 million). Its two large observatories attract over 1.5 million visitors a year.

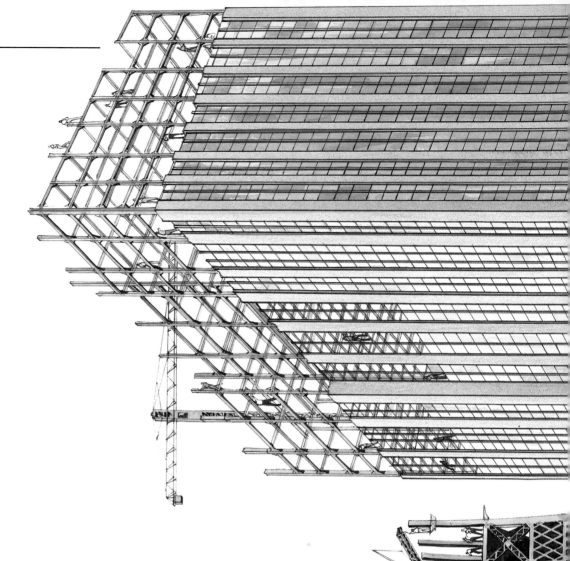

TALL TOWERS

As cities have become more crowded, land for buildings has become scarcer and its cost has risen. The only answer to this problem has been for architects to design taller and taller buildings, with many more storeys available for offices and accommodation. Today, major cities like New York, Chicago and Toronto are noticeably dominated by skyscrapers that tower above the city streets.

The first big skyscraper in the world was the Chrysler Building in New York, completed in 1930.

But its 77 storeys were soon overlooked by the 102-storey Empire State Building, completed in the same year, which held the record for the tallest unsupported building until 1974. Today, the CN Tower in Toronto is the world's tallest tower, although it is easily dwarfed by numerous television and radio masts throughout the world that are supported by guy ropes. The tallest of these is the Warszawa radio mast in Poland, which is 645m (2,117ft) tall.

The tallest in the world
Five of the six towers shown here have at one time been the tallest buildings in the world. Only the Leaning Tower of Pisa has held no such record, but it is unique in that it leans dramatically to one side.

The Eiffel Tower, Paris
Completed in 1889, the Eiffel Tower is 300m (986ft) tall, and was the world's tallest building until the construction of the Chrysler Building in 1930.

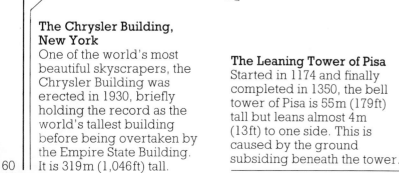
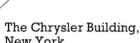

The Chrysler Building, New York
One of the world's most beautiful skyscrapers, the Chrysler Building was erected in 1930, briefly holding the record as the world's tallest building before being overtaken by the Empire State Building. It is 319m (1,046ft) tall.

The Leaning Tower of Pisa
Started in 1174 and finally completed in 1350, the bell tower of Pisa is 55m (179ft) tall but leans almost 4m (13ft) to one side. This is caused by the ground subsiding beneath the tower.

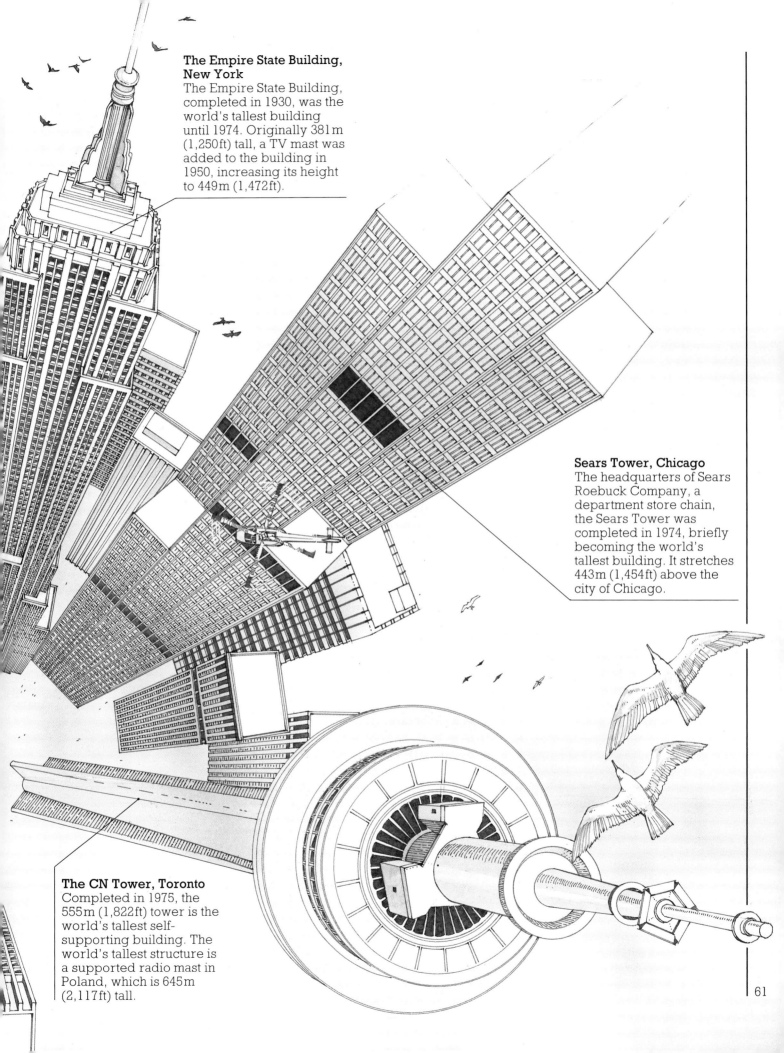

The Empire State Building, New York
The Empire State Building, completed in 1930, was the world's tallest building until 1974. Originally 381m (1,250ft) tall, a TV mast was added to the building in 1950, increasing its height to 449m (1,472ft).

Sears Tower, Chicago
The headquarters of Sears Roebuck Company, a department store chain, the Sears Tower was completed in 1974, briefly becoming the world's tallest building. It stretches 443m (1,454ft) above the city of Chicago.

The CN Tower, Toronto
Completed in 1975, the 555m (1,822ft) tower is the world's tallest self-supporting building. The world's tallest structure is a supported radio mast in Poland, which is 645m (2,117ft) tall.

THE WONDERS OF SIZE

One of the reasons the original Seven Wonders were chosen was for their size. When they were built, they were among the tallest constructions in the world, dwarfing the houses that most people lived in. Yet their size was limited by the fact that apart from wood, stone was the only available building material. As stone is heavy, a building could not be too tall or it would topple over. This meant that for centuries there was a natural limit to the height of buildings. So even though St. Peter's in Rome, the biggest church in the world, was built as late as the 16th century, it could easily fit inside the Great Pyramid, built 4,500 years before it.

But the introduction of iron and steel, then reinforced concrete in the last two centuries has made it possible to construct much taller buildings. The Eiffel Tower in Paris, the Sear's Tower in Chicago and the CN Tower in Toronto all easily overlook the original Seven Wonders of the World.

Wonders old and new
Shown with the original Seven Wonders are five more recent ones – the Leaning Tower of Pisa, St Peter's Church in Rome, the Eiffel Tower in Paris, the Sears Tower in Chicago and the CN Tower in Toronto.

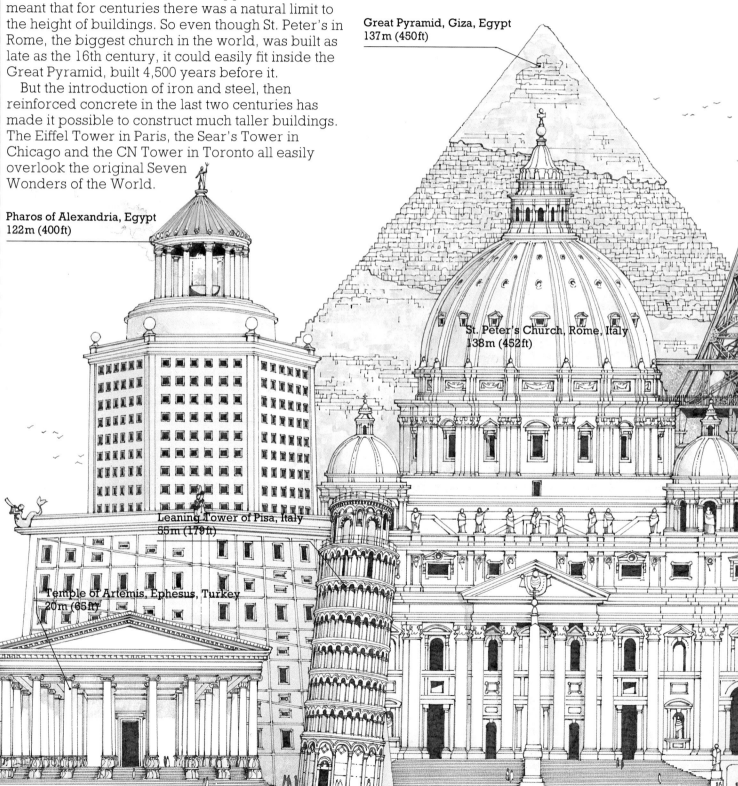

Great Pyramid, Giza, Egypt
137m (450ft)

Pharos of Alexandria, Egypt
122m (400ft)

St. Peter's Church, Rome, Italy
138m (452ft)

Leaning Tower of Pisa, Italy
55m (179ft)

Temple of Artemis, Ephesus, Turkey
20m (65ft)

Sears Tower, Chicago, U.S.A.
443m (1,454ft)

CN Tower,
Toronto, Canada
555m (1,822ft)

Eiffel Tower, Paris, France
300m (986ft)

Hanging Gardens of Babylon, Iraq
90m (300ft)

Colossus of Rhodes, Greece
37m (120ft)

Mausoleum at Halicarnassus,
Turkey 43m (140ft)

Statue of Zeus, Olympia, Greece
12m (40ft)

INDEX

Acknowledgements
Dorling Kindersley would like to thank Sandra Archer, Andrew Duncan, Martin Greenwood, Kate Hinton, David Salariya and Lynn Bresler for their help in producing this book.